HOW DOGS MAKE US BETTER HUMANS

Tails of Unconditional Love

BEA BOHM-MEYER

Dear MP:

Thank you for being such a great friend, for helping me in my transition to retirement and for sharing beautiful Josie with me.

Your friend,

ML ♡

CONTENTS

WHY WRITE THIS BOOK?

*"Dogs are whispers that speak to us when we most
need them and teach us about unconditional love."*

— BEA BOHM-MEYER

Why the heck does a person who has spent the past 20
years helping companies design their leadership presence
and corporate culture want to write a book about dogs?

It really is a good question. The most obvious answer is
that I love dogs.

This work is a passion project brought to life during the
strange days of COVID-19. The idea was inspired by all
the puppies that joined our human family, those who
became part of our new family business, The Leash Team,

and finally, by all the pups that have impacted our lives and taught us life lessons even if we didn't know it.

The book was also created as a result of a more complex and deep-rooted desire to share my lifelong learning and experiences with dogs. If you are present and if you really listen, dogs are teaching us every day. There have been so many lessons learned from our furry friends that have changed me and those around me. There have been small moments and big moments that have brought sheer joy and excruciating sorrow, bonds made with pups, and the friendships made with their hoomans. Most importantly, the lessons of unconditional love, empathy, non-judgment, and leadership. These are some of the very lessons that have made me a better human being, albeit not perfect, but better.

I have spent most of my adult life working with senior leaders, executives, and incredible teams, helping them understand themselves, their potential, and what it truly means to lead ourselves and lead others. I often ask them to look for a source of inspiration for how they want to lead their lives. I am not surprised when some have mentioned their dogs as that source of inspiration when it comes to compassion and unconditional love.

Growing up around beautiful canines and having the privilege of walking with them almost every day has made me realize there are lessons to be learned in everything and everywhere; we just need to listen. I don't want to miss these important opportunities to be present in the learning that dogs teach us every day. We spend so much time looking outward, trying to find ways to grow personally and professionally, while trying to find ways to be happy. I hope this book shows that we should not overlook something that might be right in front of us. Sometimes it is that something with a wet nose, furry belly, and big heart that shows us unconditional love and that their love helps us become better humans.

I have been passionate about dogs since I can remember. When I was a little girl, I used to dream about being surrounded by fur babies all the time. I wanted to be the Doctor Doolittle of dogs. I would even go out and buy stuffed puppy animals that looked real. I would put them on a leash and walk them down the street. Sometimes I would tell my friends the stuffed animals were real and never let them get close enough to see the truth.

When I was about 6, I begged my mom for a dog. We were Hungarian so my mom purchased a Hungarian Vizsla puppy from a farm. The poor thing had been torn away from its mother too early and was very sickly. We felt the puppy was suffering and we had to bring it back to be with its mother. It was such a sad experience, and my mother never did ask for the money back because she knew the breeder was financially challenged. Our second dog was a rescue from the Humane Society, which was called the SPCA back then. A beautiful Samoyed named Sammie. He was only with us for 24 hours. During those few hours, he chewed his way out of our yard while we were not looking. We never did see him again. He was so amazingly regal and handsome, but we shouldn't have let his good looks fool us; he was sneaky, smart, and determined. I worried about him for months and I still think about him. Both of those experiences broke my heart.

Finally, friends of our family asked my mom if we could take care of a miniature black Labrador for the summer. That was a ruse. Taking care of the dog was a trial run, as my mom wanted to see if the dog would be a fit for our family. This dog was not only a fit, but she also became an instant part of our hearts.

She brought our family closer together. My mom was strict with her. I had to vacuum every day because she shed, and she was never allowed upstairs in our bedrooms. When my mom was not looking, I would sneak her up to my bed. I think my mom knew and I appreciated that she never said anything. We named this new member of our family, Morzsa which means breadcrumbs in Hungarian because her brown eyes looked like breadcrumbs. She was so pretty. Morzsa was with us for 14 years and had a great impact on our lives. I still think of her and feel her unconditional love.

Fast forward to today. Yahoo! I am surrounded by dogs because of my husband's brand-new business, The Leash Team. My husband Dan is a serial entrepreneur. He has had three successful businesses and a few...not so much. As a successful entrepreneur, he's not averse to taking on risks and acting on opportunities. This is a man that never gives up.

Dan was forced into retirement at a time when he was going through some incredible health challenges. Over the span of 40 years, he developed this incredible noise in his head. One day, we were hiking with the family in British Columbia and were at the top of a mountain when a plane flew over us. We were near the peak of the mountain and the plane was so close, it felt like I could jump up and touch it. The family all fell to the ground and ducked as if the plane was about to hit us, and Dan just stood there. When we all stood up, Dan said, "That noise you just heard is the same kind of noise that is in my head all the time."

In the early spring of 2018, he decided to start walking dogs because he was bored of retirement. We had two dogs of our own and that's how it all started. We have an incredible river valley in Edmonton, Alberta where we live, with many off-leash parks. Friends and neighbors knew he was going every day, so they started paying him to walk their dogs. As a serial entrepreneur he saw an opportunity and within a year he was doing two walks a day, walking an average of 8 to 12 dogs each walk. Those who knew him marvelled at how much the dogs loved and responded to him. He loved those dogs so much that he got his certification in behavior modification and training methodology. He was incredible to watch. He would be walking down a path with a dozen dogs and stop at a fork in the road. Sometimes he would just nod his head which way to go, and the dogs would go in that direction. I swear sometimes he just thought of the direction and the dogs knew where to go.

It was during this time that he received two life-changing cochlear implants to help him with the noise in his head and his hearing. It was a long journey, and his quality of life finally started to improve. I truly believe that without the dogs, he wouldn't have made it through all of his challenges as well as he did.

In March of 2020, COVID-19 became the new reality. You would think the dog walking business would have taken a big hit, and it kind of did. But Dan was extraordinary. For those people who still had to work but couldn't afford the dog walks, he did it for free or at a reduced rate. For frontline workers, he would occasionally give free dog walks to honor them for being heroes.

I started to realize that there's something special about this business. People love their dogs and when *you* love their dogs, they love you! Many of our clients became our close friends. When the pandemic restrictions allowed for it, we were invited to dinners, BBQs, and special events, and on summer days, you would find clients sitting on our deck having a glass of wine.

As an entrepreneur and builder, Dan saw an opportunity to create jobs and grow a business based on his passion for dogs. Instead of riding out COVID-19, he decided to harness it and hire young, educated people who were passionate about dogs. He created an extensive dog walking certification program, canine protocols, and a culture that meant all staff and clients were family. The business has grown since the beginning of the pandemic and today, The Leash Team walks approximately 300 dogs each week - in groups of 6 to 8 dogs per walker. Dan is always eager to share that each day the dogs "teach us something special about ourselves and there is nothing like it."

As I've learned so much through all these experiences, I wanted to share some of the most meaningful stories and lessons with the rest of the world, or at least those who would listen. This book is an informal journey of people who surround me. It is not a literary piece. It is not an academic piece. It is a collection of dog stories from the heart. I have written from my own experiences and documented the experiences of others.

I have included a 12-page personal journal toward the end of the book, allowing you to document your own stories and lessons learned. It is one way to honour the lessons and cherish the memories.

GRATITUDE

To everyone who is part of this book, thank you from the bottom of my heart. It has been a great honor to collaborate with you and it was fun! I hope that people reading these stories will be more present and live with more unconditional love in their lives. I truly hope this book inspires us to have a bit more connection and compassion in the world, not only with our dogs, but with each other.

I want to thank all my family and friends for their love and support, and for being part of this journey. Thank you to my friend and colleague, Steve Brierley from the *Better Human Group*, who encouraged me to be the voice, to make what is invisible visible, and for giving me little choice but to write this book. Thank you to Hillary Rideout, also of the *Better Human Group*, for tirelessly working with me on bringing this book to life. You were relentless and supportive all at the same time.

Big hugs and thanks to the people and pups who shared their stories with us. Thanks to Mary K MacDonald who agreed to edit this book and to Ronda Nedelec and Vicky Andress who agreed to do the final read. All three supported this project out of grace and love and believed in me. Sometimes that is all it takes to make things happen. Thanks to all *The Leash Team* staff, family, and pups for your inspiration to show the world that dogs do make us better humans. Love you all.

Finally, this book was born in a time of great tragedy and sacrifice. Thank you to all the frontline workers in all industries for your unconditional commitment to save lives and support life during the COVID-19 pandemic. We will never forget your determination and sacrifice.

OUR RESEARCH

As I started writing, it became clear that to get to the heart of the matter, I needed others to share their stories. So, to get data straight from the "dog's mouth," we sent out a survey with several questions to dog lovers. It was a huge success, with so many people providing us direct access to their thoughts and experiences. Due to the overwhelming number of responses to the survey, we've included a selection of comments we received about dogs and their humans in the summary of the research, which can be found in the appendix of this book. I've included two of the questions that elicited my favourite responses here.

DO YOU THINK DOGS HAVE A PURPOSE?

Family, friends, and even strangers, shared repeatedly that they experience unconditional love from their dogs, and they think *that* is a dog's purpose.

I found it interesting that the same theme of unconditional love popped up not only for this survey question, but also in the responses to many of the other survey questions.

The evidence is clear. From our research and the stories that follow, dogs touch our lives in many ways, and there seems to be one common denominator: a love that shows up without boundaries, without conditions, and without strings attached. This love from dogs appears to consistently demonstrate a type of purity and loyalty, and at times, exuberance. In analyzing the survey data and interviewing the storytellers, it also appears that a dog's love not only *touches* us, it also *teaches* us.

I want to believe with all my heart that dogs have been put on this earth to help us love and to help us learn about love. The stories that follow are real and a wonderful way to showcase that "special canine love."

WHAT HAS BEEN YOUR GREATEST REWARD AS A DOG OWNER?

Not surprisingly, happiness, affection, and unconditional love were the most mentioned responses to the question, *What has been your greatest reward as a dog owner?* The heart on the next page is a touching image of the other words most used to respond to this question.

Cuddle   Friend

Happiness   Loyalty

Companionship

Unconditional Love

Passion   **Affection**

Joy

Life

What has been your greatest reward as a dog owner?

INCREDIBLE STORIES OF HOW DOGS MAKE US BETTER HUMANS

Bea's Amazing Stories

I NEVER WANTED A DOG - WELL YES, I DID. THANK YOU, LIAM

Story 1 - Determination

"Our greatest weakness as human beings are those times when we give up. Our greatest joys are those times when we don't."

— BEA BOHM-MEYER

---

*A*nd so, the story goes...you know the situation when you have young kids, and they want a dog. You know in your heart you want a dog too. But here's the truth. You have two kids that are in school, and they play sports after school. I own my own business, my husband owns his own business, we have elderly parents, and so on and on and on. You get the gist. Where does a dog fit in? And the even bigger question is: Who is going to take care of the dog?!

Yep, I could see it with my eyes closed. Everyone would be all-in for the first 2 weeks and then I would become "Dog Mom." I would have another business that I would not be paid for... Poop Patrol. Of course, I would get more exercise, but resent that I would be alone with this furball.... although cute, the furball was not supposed to be mine. Yep, that was the story in my head, and I know I was right because I am one of the smartest people in the world. If you do not believe me, ask my mom. Yet, we all know how the story ends.

It all began when Danielle, my daughter, was in elementary school. The requests came fast and furious. "I want a puppy." "I want a dog." "Maybe just a little dog." "We must have a dog." "Please, can I have a dog?" We finally talked her into maybe looking at adopting a cat, thinking it would be much easier taking care of a cat. In time, she finally acquiesced.

We chose a weekend to go out to the adoption agencies and look at kitties. For some doggone reason - no pun intended - she didn't connect with any of the purring fur balls up for adoption. On our way home we dropped into a pet store. During those days you could still buy a pet from a pet store. Yes, I know: bad, bad, bad. I know better now. We came across two beautiful Persian kittens. They were sisters. Danielle picked up one of those kittens and it pawed at her face, and they instantly became connected. I almost dropped to the floor when the $700 price tag was gently revealed by the store manager. What happened to free kitties?

My husband Dan would have nothing to do with that. He took the young manager into the back of the store to negotiate something more reasonable. I never did find out how much he paid for that cat. I still don't want to know. You know what dads will do for their daughters...ANYTHING!

Danielle named the kitten Coco Chanel. We loved her so much that we went back to get her sister. We could not stand thinking of Coco Chanel's sister being alone. Thank goodness she was already adopted! We saved the price tag on that beautiful fur ball. You will see a pattern throughout my stories. Our family is full of bleeding hearts and we make no apologies for it.

Coco Channel was with us for 17 years even though we hardly ever saw her. She was an indoor cat, scared of everything, particularly humans of the male gender. She lived in Danielle's room and came out only to say hi to me. One of the most interesting things about Coco Chanel was that although she did not like men and stayed away from them, she loved my dad. Every time my father came over, she would come downstairs and sit on the arm of his chair. My dad had dementia and it was extraordinary just watching them sit for hours together. It reminded me that love comes in all shapes and sizes, including just "being." Not doing, just *being*. Being together, being silent, being us. It is part of the human condition that we forget about sometimes – just *being*.

On a side note, before Coco Channel passed, she caught a mouse in our house. It freaked us all out because we had never had a mouse in our house before. At least she got one in before going to kitty heaven. Anyway, this story is suppose to be our journey to dog-hood.

When my son Liam was about 12 years old, he started to bring up the question again. "When are we going to get a dog?" We talked about the responsibility of having a dog and the time we would need to ensure that it was well-loved and cared for. We explained that we just did not have the time to devote to a dog. He was not buying any of it. He promised he would walk the dog every day and he promised he would take care of it. Liam got quite frustrated with us and pivoted, approaching us with a new and different strategy.

On my desk every few days, I would get an article about having a dog. Some articles would talk about the joys of adopting a dog, some would provide data about how dogs helped people be happier, some would provide evidence that people lived longer if they had a dog, and some said people who have dogs are healthier. There was one article in particular I really loved. Liam had photocopied the Harvard Business Review (HBR) title and pasted it onto a (non-HBR) article explaining that couples with dogs have lower divorce rates. He thought HBR would impress me, and it did. I respected his ingenuity and determination. We would have the conversation about adopting a dog repeatedly and it would lead to an argument almost daily. He would say, "I want a dog." and I would bark back (no pun intended), "We're not getting a dog." Over time, I did feel this issue was starting to divide us.

One evening, Liam came to me, and I was ready for the argument. I didn't even let him open his mouth before I blurted out "We are not getting a dog. You are too busy with hockey. We are never home. We don't have time for a dog!" Liam's response was slow, intentional, and piercing. "Okay Mom, I hear you loud and clear. We are not getting a dog." Then he went on to say one simple statement that changed our lives forever.

"Mom, I just want you to know that somewhere in a dark cold room there is a puppy on a cement floor, alone, afraid and shivering. The only thing stopping it from being loved is you."

I'm going to say it. I know I shouldn't say it, but what a f***er! My heart dropped and I broke out into tears. I looked at him and said, "Go get your *freakin* dog!" I said it lovingly of course...I think.

Liam immediately turned around and, out of the corner of my eye, I saw my husband and I realized they were in cahoots together. Moments later, as they left the house, I realized they had already picked out a dog.

There are so many lessons to be learned from this experience, but I think the most important is the power of determination. My son wanted a dog so much, he would do anything to make it happen, including guilting me.

He did a pretty good job, especially because I am stubborn. I did love all the articles he left me. They were informative. Just so you know, having a dog does lead to no divorce in our family; my husband and I have been married for 30 years. The article was right!!!

I know we are not all in a position to say yes to a dog. In this case, we did say yes. Lesson learned: don't give up on your dreams. Keep pushing your mom until she breaks. We all need to follow our dreams. This childhood experience built the confidence and courage to fight for what Liam wanted. With true determination, every win brings us one step closer to realizing our full potential and owning our power.

HOW DOGS MAKE US BETTER HUMANS

This experience taught Liam the rewards of not giving up. It forced him to be creative and relentless. His determination and ingenuity paid off. We are a family that has experienced a lifetime of dog love because of Liam's determination. We are a better family for it. Thank you, Liam.

SHE SAW THE WORLD THROUGH ME

Story 2 - Empathy

"Empathy is seeing the world through the eyes of others and feeling their heart."

— BEA BOHM-MEYER

---

*C*harlie grew up with our family. It has been more than two years since she went to doggy heaven. Charlie came to us because my son guilted us into getting a dog. It was one of the best things we've ever done. I will always be thankful for Liam and his ingenuity, intelligible deceitfulness, and perseverance in not giving up on the quest for a dog. Charlie was an extraordinary dog. She was part Border Collie and part Maremma. Border Collies are great at herding sheep, cows, dogs, and even humans, and this breed loves to be working all the time. The Maremma is like an Italian mountain dog and lives to protect; that is their biggest purpose in life. Typically, in the mountains of Italy, the puppies are thrown into the herd of sheep and as they grow up, their sole job is to protect the herd from wild animals.

Charlie was living both breeds to a tee. There were times we were in our family room, and she would herd us into a corner without us even knowing it. Other times, I would take a break from work and meet the family for a walk in the river valley on the off-leash trails. When it was time for me to leave and go back to work, Charlie would try to herd us into a circle. When that did not work, she would drop to the ground and lay there with a tenacious disposition that resembled, might I say it, my own stubbornness. She was an obedient dog but incredibly stubborn. When we called her, she would stay and not move until the family came together again. I had to stop meeting the family for walks on the days when I had to go back to work, for fear that Charlie would sit in the park all day until I came back.

Walks became a family function; we did it together and we did it often. I will truly be grateful for Charlie and this gift in particular. Families are often so busy being pulled in different directions by different things and we were one of those families. I honestly believe we would have lost our family connection if it wasn't for Charlie. Even today, although she may not be with us in fur body, she's still with us in fur spirit. We still go for family walks with our other dogs even though our children are now fully grown adults. It is a gift that keeps on giving. We will give it to our grandchildren as well one day; you know the ones? The grandchildren I am still waiting for.

Dogs connect us in many ways, not just physically. Charlie connected our family emotionally, and we are closer for it. I also believe undeniably Charlie helped me become a better and more present human being.

She helped me connect with my inner soul and human consciousness. This, I didn't see coming.

Charlie possessed this intuition that could not only read a room but could predict your next action. For instance, on many occasions, I would be working at my computer, and I would think "It's time to go for a walk." To be clear, I did not say it aloud, I did not get up, I did not put on my walking pants, and I did not do anything physical that would indicate I wanted to go for a walk. It was just a thought, and as soon as I had that thought, Charlie would come running into my office almost every time. It was remarkable. I knew I was developing a very deep connection with her; I just didn't realize how deep until a few important occurrences started me thinking about connection and empathy; feeling what others feel.

OCCURRENCE #1

My father and I were remarkably close. When my kids were little, he was given a second chance at life when he was gifted a new heart from a donor and their family. If you are out there reading this, please know that you gave my dad the opportunity to love his grandbabies. You also gave my mom, my sister, and me, an additional ten years with him. It was an extraordinary and selfless gift. Unfortunately, nothing lasts forever and one day, I got the phone call from my mom, or maybe it was my sister, I can't remember. All I heard was that my dad had passed and at that moment, I felt so empty and alone. I remember standing up from my chair; my body felt heavy, and my mind felt dark. I started to walk down the stairs and when I got to the bottom, Charlie approached me. She jumped up on me, which she normally never did. She put her paws around my waist and snuggled her head downwards into my tummy. We sat there for about 5 minutes while my husband just watched. He did not know what to do. I don't even think he knew what was going on. He was just in awe of the moment. For me, it was like Charlie was the only one in the world who knew what I was feeling. Charlie was always so present to me and my needs. That day she saw me and she felt my pain.

OCCURRENCE #2

When I walked with Charlie in our beautiful river valley, sometimes it was a joy and sometimes it was stressful because occasionally, she would be grumpy to the other dogs. I began to think that maybe she needed some additional training. Then my kids said to me, "It's not her mom, it's you." What the heck???! Yet, they were right. You see, when I was walking in a stressed or grumpy state, Charlie would read my energy and she would in turn, be grumpy to the other dogs. If I was happy and joyful, she was a dream to walk; she was very social and gentle and there were no issues. She was deeply connected to me, and I realized that my energy, my thoughts, and my actions 100% impacted her. Charlie reminded me I was in my head too much when I was stressed, which disconnected me from others. This made me sad, as I realized during these times, I was impacting my kids. She showed me that life is good when I am present and connected to the world, not only with my head, but also with my heart. During these times the trees seemed greener, the sun brighter and walks happier. I became more curious with the people around me and even more patient when others were grumpy. I became more present to all the energy around me. I became connected.

It took the relationship with Charlie to remind me that our interactions with others are defined by how we show up in the world. Whether it be with words or thoughts or our energy, we directly impact the people around us, including our dogs. That impact defines our relationships and our connections with others. Charlie was living evidence of this concept. My lesson from this was to become more reflective and conscious about how I feel about myself and how I make others feel. Charlie helped me become very present in how I show up in the world and how I must be curious about what others are feeling and experiencing. Today I practice conscious empathy and I endeavor to see the world through the eyes of others. This is truly a gift. If you ever have read anything about emotional intelligence, you will understand that the essence and foundation of our success and our relationships are founded in our emotional intelligence, our empathy, and our intuition. I now truly understand that how we feel about ourselves is a mirror of how we treat other people. In the end, it wasn't a book or a mentor that taught me this, it was my Charlie.

My heart is still broken because Charlie is no longer with us, however, she left me a much better and more conscious person. Charlie helped me to connect to the world in a more meaningful way. It is a wonderful way to live. Thank you, Charlie. I love you.

HOW DOGS MAKE US BETTER HUMANS

Life with Charlie taught me the true meaning of being present, as well as empathy; seeing the world through the eyes of others. She gave me grace when I needed it and held up a mirror by mimicking my behavior when grace was not good enough. With kindness and love, she taught me to get out of my head and live in the here and now. I am now deeply conscious that energy matters and our actions and words will either connect us or divide us.

BETTER TO HAVE LOVED AND LOST, THAN NOT TO HAVE LOVED AT ALL

Story 3 - Keep Your Heart Open

"Dogs can heal a broken heart and show you the way back to a life that must be lived."

— BEA BOHM-MEYER

*Y*ears before my husband and I started our dog walking business, The Leash Team, there was Charlie. As you know, I never really wanted Charlie. Well, I did but our household was so busy I didn't think it would be a good idea. In the end, it was 3 against me. So, Charlie was in.

When she arrived, she was still a puppy; full of piss and vinegar and stubborn as all %$#@. In addition to her energy, Charlie decided independently that there was no way she would be crate trained. Ugh! When we put her in the crate, she would either eat through the plastic wall or chew on her leg until the raw flesh poked through. Can you imagine that?! The irony is that although my husband Dan, and our children, Liam, and Danielle, really wanted this dog, Charlie spent a lot of time at home with me. Liam was going to school and playing hockey every day. Danielle was going to school and playing soccer most days. Dan was an entrepreneur and traveled with his business. Here I was, left to raise this beautiful dog that was not supposed to be mine. She was the epitome of a Border Collie-Maremma; a herder and a protector. When she looked into my eyes, I felt like she could read my soul. I was so falling in love with her. I could feel my heart hurt every time I was away from her. We were connected in a very special way.

One Monday afternoon following one of my out-of-home-office meetings, I found myself close to the Humane Society. I don't know why or how it happened. I had no intention of visiting the dog shelter. Yet my car magically drove into their parking lot. I had been thinking about Charlie and not wanting her to be alone in the house when I was out attending meetings. Although I did work from home a fair bit, there were days I left early in the morning, leaving Charlie alone for the better part of the day. I sat in the car on that day watching the people and dogs walk in and out of the shelter. I kept thinking, "What am I doing here?"

I knew exactly what I was doing. Charlie needed a brother, or a sister and I was going to make it happen. No more lonely mornings for Charlie if I had anything to do with it.

Can you guess what happened next? I got out of my car. Hesitantly I walked into the shelter. There were so many dogs. I have always been a bleeding heart and have always wanted to help save the world in my own way. On that day, at that moment, I just wanted to save all those puppies. My heart was filled with so much love. I couldn't help but wonder why these innocent fur balls didn't have someone special to care for them.

As I walked through the hallways, I stumbled across a beautiful and very scared Border Collie. She was 2 years old and the opposite color of Charlie; all black with some white. I immediately called Dan who, with a surprise in his voice, asked where I was calling from. I told him there was a Border Collie at the dog shelter that would make a great companion for Charlie and that he should come for an introduction. I don't think he even hung up the phone before he got into the car. He arrived within 20 minutes. By the time he got to the shelter, the dog had been adopted. It was crazy. I was so sad and yet I was happy for her.

We ended up walking around for about half an hour when Dan saw two puppies, a boy and a girl. They had been found on the side of the road. The rescuers thought they might have been thrown out of a car window. I think there were more puppies, but they did not survive. Dan walked into that room and this small little thing jumped into his arms. The Humane Society had named this little puppy Buckley. Dan and I always lovingly argue about who picked who. He thinks he picked Buckley, but I can remember it so well. Buckley picked him.

Although I initiated the addition to our family, I wasn't prepared for a puppy. He was so handsome. A mix of Border Collie, Hound, and Saint Bernard...we think. We still do not know to this day. I was also worried about Charlie, who was now almost 2 years old. Would she like the idea of a fur ball baby running around her house. As Dan tried to talk me into the adoption, the only way I would agree is if we introduced Charlie to this little bundle. I needed to know Charlie would like him and that she would be okay. Dan immediately drove back home to get Charlie. I stayed and was escorted into a waiting room.

While I waited for Dan to come back, I talked to one of the staff members about Buckley's sister. I said if this introduction is successful, I'd like to adopt her as well. Yes, I said it out loud. What was wrong with me?! I am a bleeding heart. Well, if I wanted to save the world, dogs are a big part of the world, I rationalized to myself. 1 dog or 3 dogs, what is the difference? 1 puppy, 2 puppies… what is the big deal? WHAT IS WRONG WITH ME??? This is the momma that didn't even want a dog. Yet, I couldn't imagine leaving Buckley's sister in that room all alone while we drove home.

After some time, Buckley was brought to the room and introduced to Charlie. It did not go well. Charlie did not like Buckley one little bit. She ignored him, had a few growls, and kept walking away, all the while looking at me like, "What are we doing here?" Or so I thought. Well, that was the story in my head. I was worried she was going to bite him.

The rest I don't remember very well. The last thing I heard was Dan saying, "Perfect, they love each other. We will take him." Then he signed the papers while I was still in shock. Did we see the same thing? And then I heard myself say it...I told myself not to open my mouth, but I heard myself say it... "And we will adopt Buckley's sister too." Dan looked at me like I was out of my mind and hugged me and said, "Okay. I really love you."

Despite my unexpected decision, by the time we signed all the adoption papers, Buckley's sister had already been adopted by a wonderful family with young children. We introduced ourselves and wished each other good luck. We did see that family one more time in the dog park, but Buckley's sister wasn't with them. They were crate training her and had left her at home.

The days and months to come were difficult. Charlie did not appreciate this little puppy in her home. She desperately tried to ignore him, snapping at him every chance she got. I could see he tried so hard to vie for her love. It took a year but eventually, something happened, and they became inseparable.

As I reflect on that first year, a few things became clear. Our biggest downfall as human beings is that sometimes we don't see things that are not black and white and some-times things are not as they appear.

Charlie wasn't annoyed with Buckley (very much); she was schooling him. Not only was she teaching him to be a dog, but she was also teaching him to be a *good* dog. When we went to the park, Charlie would play with Buckley until Buckley got too rough. Then she put him in his place. When they walked the trails, Charlie would not let Buckley pass her. This wasn't ego, it was a lesson. Eventually, they walked side by side every walk. Their journey together was extraordinary. They were not only siblings, they also became best friends. They looked out for each other, they played with each other, they slept with each other, and they walked the beautiful trails in our river valley together.

Even now when I am in the dog park and experience dogs growling, I know it is most likely not aggression. Dogs school each other. That is how they learn.

The year Charlie turned 10 years old, Dan and I took a trip to Ireland. We got a frantic phone call in the middle of the night from our daughter letting us know that Charlie was sick. She was given two blood transfusions during the next 6 weeks. It was cancer and it was relentless, and the moment came when we had to let her go. We were with her in her final moments. It was Good Friday. Dan brought a turkey dinner to the hospital where Buckley and Charlie ate their last meal together. Then, in a moment, darkness was upon our whole family. It was f***ing awful.

When we got home Buckley wouldn't move and wouldn't eat. He did the strangest thing the next morning. While we were asleep, we heard something scraping the floor downstairs. We got up only to see that every floor vent in the house had been taken out and turned upside down. I went into the living room and Buckley was taking out the last vent. I burst into tears. It was as if a knife went through my heart. Buckley had never done that before, but Charlie did. It was something Charlie did all the time when she was hot. When Charlie couldn't sleep, she would scratch out the floor vents to get more air coming at her.

What did this mean? Was he trying to tell us something? Was this the way he grieved? Was it Charlie talking through Buckley? I couldn't even imagine how broken Buckley must have felt. We still can't believe to this day that he did that. He never did it before her death and he never did it after that morning. Buckley did not eat for days, and I thought, will he ever be the same?

Charlie's death changed him. He was never the same after she left us. *We* were never the same after she left us. They were family dogs, yet Charlie was Liam's dog, Buckley was Danielle's dog, and they were both our dogs, but Charlie at that time, was my heart and soul.

Ten days after Charlie passed away, Dan came home with a little black and white puppy. By this time The Leash Team was up and running. I thought he brought this dog home to be socialized. I still was mourning Charlie and didn't have the energy to be excited. Ironically this little puppy looked like Charlie and that made things even worse.

All my assumptions were wrong. Dan went out and got a puppy to try to heal our broken hearts. I was so angry and told him he had to take the dog back right away. I couldn't even look at that little thing. She was so full of love and so scared of her new surroundings. But I didn't care. I didn't want anything to do with her. I was angry and I wasn't ready to open my heart to another dog. It was too soon.

Dan said he phoned the home where he had gotten the puppy and arranged to return her at 2:00 pm the next day. I tried desperately not to have anything to do with her, but she was so loving. I watched her play on the floor and told myself not to get too attached. I was watching one of my favorite TV shows called *Blue Bloods*. It is a show about a family of police officers in New York City. In the show, there is a character named Eddie. She is a young, beautiful, and smart cop. I thought to myself, if we were to keep this puppy, I would love to call her Eddie. It was a boy's name for a girl, just like Charlie was a boy's name for our girl. As the evening went on, I knew in my heart that puppy would stay with us forever.

When Dan got ready to take her back the next day, I stopped him. I knew right then he never phoned. He never had any intention of taking her back.

Poor Buckley. He was now saddled with this puppy we called Eddie. And as Charlie seemed not to like Buckley, Buckley seemed not to like Eddie. In fact, we had a problem because he was very jealous. At one point he bit Eddie's head and damaged her eye. Eventually, I saw Buckley start to school Eddie. Don't play too rough, don't run around the house, don't sleep on my bed. Buckley was not as gentle as Charlie in his teaching methodology, but I don't think he had very much choice as Eddie grew to be an

80-pound puppy. In the end, Buckley did a great job of raising Eddie.

I too had a hard time loving Eddie. She was such a good puppy and a great dog, but my heart was broken because of Charlie, until something strange happened. It was time for Eddie to get another set of her shots. The veterinarian asked me how I was doing. I told her that my heart was still broken, and I missed Charlie so much. I was trying so hard with Eddie, but the connection was not the same. She grabbed my hand, looked deep into my eyes, and said, "Try harder because Eddie is trying so hard for you." I couldn't believe it. I looked at her confused and angry. She said again, "I'm serious, that dog is working hard for you."

I turned the corner that day and became more present with Eddie and, as my heart opened for her, she gave me so many gifts. Buckley schooled Eddie; Eddie schooled me. She taught me that I can love another, she showed me I can walk in the river valley again. She hugged me just as hard as Charlie did but differently. She loved me just as much as Charlie, but in her way. She was way more forgiving of my energy when I was grumpy. And most of all she taught me it was okay to laugh again. She is a goofball and at the same time, she is a gentle giant. And together we embarked on many adventures and many belly giggles.

How blessed we are to have had so many wonderful experiences with all our dogs. Today Eddie and Buckley are the best of friends.

HOW DOGS MAKE US BETTER HUMANS

This experience taught me so many meaningful lessons. Buckley and Eddie were there for me when I did not want to let go. They were patient and kind. I am grateful to Buckley who raised Eddie when I could not. In the end, they both taught me that letting go is not forgetting. Letting go is to open your heart to new possibilities, new experiences, and new kinds of love. It was the experience of their unconditional love that allowed me to heal and open my heart again. I believe an open heart is the true journey of our human spirit. Thank you, Charlie, Buckley, and Eddie, for loving me without judgment.

HOW BUCKLEY AND EDDIE SHOW UP IN THE WORLD

Story 4 - Purpose

"Purpose is the expression of ourselves to the world."

— BEA BENKOVA (*BEA'S MENTOR FROM EUROPE*)

---

*S*o today, here I sit watching my husband build this beautiful business around dogs, called The Leash Team. It is like he is living my childhood dream. No one is doing quite what he is doing. He is dedicated, passionate, and has a really smart team. Yes, I am on the team too, however, I am not a dog walker. Apparently, I worry too much, and it affects the dogs. He walks groups of dogs off-leash on the trails and in the parks of our beautiful city. It's amazing to experience. In my heart, I feel it allows dogs to be dogs. They sniff with freedom, explore with wonderment, socialize with each other, which builds their confidence, and they get a ton of exercise, running and frolicking together. It's an extraordinary way to spend an afternoon whether you are canine or human. The dogs and clients are like family. And, speaking of family, Buckley, and Eddie, our two current family dogs have important roles in this company. They are both Directors of Client Engagement.

I often wonder why God put dogs on earth. These beautiful, furry, open-hearted creatures that embrace life are a good example of how to live a good life. They are a gift to humanity. Do you ever wonder if dogs have a specific purpose?

During this time of COVID-19, there are so many furry babies being adopted. We call them the COVID-19 puppies. They have allowed families to focus on nurturing and connection rather than the emptiness and disconnection from the rest of society. Is that their purpose? To remind us human types of how important *connection* is to the survival of human happiness, prosperity, creativity, and love?

As I drink my coffee this morning and watch my two pups, I cannot help but question if they know their purpose. Is it a bigger purpose that they all have in common as part of being canine? Or is it an individual purpose that they must contribute to this world because each dog is special, and each dog has some unique talent or behavioural trait to offer. Not so different from us humans.

My heart is filled with joy as I remember raising my dogs. Charlie did not like "puppy" Buckley and bit his face to school him, letting him know he was annoying. Buckley, our second dog, did not like "puppy" Eddie, our third dog, and bit her face to school her when she was annoying. Unfortunately, that bite caused more damage than expected, as Eddie almost lost her eye. In the end, Charlie loved Buckley and when Charlie passed, Buckley fell in love with Eddie. They love each other like brother and sister and became the best of friends.

Each of our dogs is unique and have brought different gifts to our family. I wrote a bit about Charlie earlier. She could read me and my energy. I loved her so much and felt a special connection. She helped me interpret the world. Now, let me share with you a bit about Buckley and Eddie.

In the beginning, our second dog Buckley, was an exuberant puppy with a strong spirit and was a force to be reckoned with. We did not know if we could ever harness his energy. Yet as he grew older, he turned into this incredibly wise soul. We would take him for walks to the dog park and people would stop and ask us what kind of dog Buckley was. We never really had an answer because he was a rescue. We would share that he was part Hound, part Border Collie, part Saint Bernard, but every part of him was pure love. Not a word of a lie. Most of the conversations ended up with people saying that Buckley had this intense stare. It almost seemed he could see into the depths of your soul. Funny talk for a dog park conversation, but it kept happening. I feel he just seems to live in the present moment, and he is also present with the person he is with.

As Buckley grew older it seemed he grew even wiser. Our friends would come over and ask if they could adopt him. We knew one couple who had just adopted a dog. In fact, we encouraged the adoption. They were going through the trials and tribulations of their new circumstances. You know that stage. The stage where you do not understand why your dog has a mind of its own and is not afraid to use it. My friend at one point looked at me and said, "Can I trade my dog for Buckley?" I smiled and hugged her and said, "You do not mean that." She did not. Then I said, "I have gone through what you're going through. I'm not about to give up my reward which, is a well-trained healthy dog who is now my best friend." I am happy to report that my friend has a love affair with her pup, and it is beautiful to watch.

Buckley is now 8 years old and has developed a love affair with outdoor adventures. Yes, *adventures*. My daughter and her new husband take Buckley on many trips to the mountains. They hike, ice fish, go boating, and camp. Buckley even has his own backpack. I also believe Buckley thinks the camping tent is set up just for him. You can just see his excitement when preparing for a trip. He loves to be outdoors. Buckley now spends half his time at my daughter's house. Although Danielle loves Eddie to the moon, she has a special bond with Buckley. They share the same interests and have the same temperament. When she has a bad day, he is there for her. When she has a great day, he is there for her. The love is unconditional. We tease her husband that when he married Danielle, he also married Buckley.

I do not like to share Buckley, but I also do not want a custody battle on my hands. LOL!!!! Although we co-parent, I kind of feel that Buckley thinks Danielle's house is his vacation house and on occasion, his sister Eddie goes for sleepovers as well. What a life! It is true what they say, it's a dog's life!!!!

I should mention that when Buckley is not adventuring, he is working hard for The Leash Team. He is the dog at the end of the line, watching and observing to ensure no dog falls behind. He is also the boss dog that helps keep everyone in line.

On the other hand, as much as Eddie loves to visit Danielle's house, she thrives being at our home and walking with The Leash Team. It is kind of like Eddie has her own adventures every day. It appears she thinks she is the boss. Eddie, on her own, has developed a training procedure on the walks that is quite interesting. It is her way of protecting the newcomers. I would like to take the credit for training her to do it, but I cannot. Eddie instinctively does this all on her own.

When The Leash Team brings a new dog on the walks, these newbies are put on a training lead. Because the walks are all off-leash, The Leash Team keeps them on the long lead until they feel comfortable that the dog has developed good recall habits and will return on command. Until they can prove they have a strong recall, the dog drags the long lead which is like dragging a very long leash.

Eddie always watches the new dogs and if they get too far away, she will grab the long lead with her mouth and bring them back closer to the group. Sometimes she does not even drop the lead. Sometimes she takes it and the dog for a walk herself. I wonder if she feels it is her responsibility to train the dogs to fall in line with the rest of the group. Or maybe she desires to protect them. Eddie is part Pyrenees. The breed is termed "a gentle giant," which she is most of the time. Yet do not let that fool you. When there is a threat, there is no gentle, only giant. We experienced this when a stranger came to our doorstep very late one evening. We did not know his intentions and the stranger did not stay long. I was even a bit frightened of how Eddie showed up at that moment. I am certain she feels responsible for protecting us and the group of dogs on their off-leash walks.

When Eddie is not helping walking dogs on the long lead, she is instigating play. She leads the dogs through the trails, tempts them playfully with sticks, and asks them to chase her. Imagine this big goofy, lovable, giant white dog "Play Bowing" to pups and people alike. Eddie is a professional at the Play Bow, a language used by dogs inviting all to come and play.

As Buckley has a special bond with my daughter, Eddie has a special bond with my son. She always looks for him when she comes home from her walks. Many times, I find her downstairs cuddled up on his bed as the two of them sleep in a peaceful and cozy slumber. When we let Eddie outside from the upstairs door, many times she wants to be let in downstairs by Liam. I often find them on the floor together, chatting and hugging. Eddie gives the best hugs. Liam is the cool person in her life that secretly spoils her. They are two peas in a pod and have an unbreakable bond.

I love the fact that my children are grown up and they still cherish the dogs. This canine love is an unconditional love that bonds our family in ways that are different from human connection. I did not say it is better, just different. We laugh when each of us travels. The phone calls home start with, "How are the dogs?" Then we ask, "How are you?" At least our family knows the priorities.

My mom, who is Grandma to the dogs, looks forward to their visits. She lives in a retirement residence. The dogs know where she lives and how to get into her building. They get just as excited when we mention Grandma's name as *she* does when we tell her the dogs are coming. Sometimes the 3 of them don't even know I am in the same room with them. I'm okay with that. I love that my mom feels these fur balls are like her children. I love that the dogs cherish her and the time they spend together. I think every seniors home should have a dog.

Like many human families, do we put dogs first in some circumstances? I wonder, do we treat our dogs better than we treat our family, our friends, our colleagues, or our workmates? It's an interesting question. All I know is when the dogs are around, we feel we are more present to every-one's love. When the dogs are around, we are more forgiv-ing, lighter, more conscious of what is occurring for us.

HOW DOGS MAKE US BETTER HUMANS

And as for the question, do dogs have a purpose?

We know each pup is different. They come in all shapes, sizes, and breeds and they have unique personalities and different talents. Buckley is wise and soulful and lives in the present moment. Eddie is social, goofy, loving, and is also a protector. What they both have in common is uncon-ditional love. This seems to be the commonality amongst all dogs.

I do believe dogs have a greater purpose. I believe they've been put on this earth to teach us so many things that all start with unconditional love. The challenge is, are we smart enough to listen? If we treated everyone we touched the same way we treated our dogs (and I am talking to the dog lovers here), would this world be a better and kinder place to live? You know the answer. Here's to the dogs and the important lessons we can learn from their true purpose... teaching us unconditional love in their own unique way.

LET'S TALK DOGS, NOT FOOTBALL

Story 5 - To Serve

"To serve is humanity's greatest opportunity. Why do dogs do it better?"

— BEA BOHM-MEYER

I reached out to my friend, Len Rhodes, because I knew he and his partner, Maureen MacKay, were crazy about dogs.

I first met Len when he was the CEO of the Edmonton CFL football team. Len has had a great career in sports, and I wanted to talk to him about growing high-performance company cultures. He seemed like such a nice guy and very approachable, so I took a chance and emailed him. In my email, I invited myself up to his office and he welcomed me with open arms.

I will never forget walking into that office. His big smile was enough to make me feel comfortable immediately. You know the feeling when you can see someone's heart right away? Then there was that floor-to-ceiling window that overlooked the green and gold chairs in the football stadium. It was stunning, grand, and impactful. Len invited me to sit. The first question he asked before I even made it to the chair was, "Do you like football?" I wanted to lie because I wanted him to like me, but I could not. I very honestly and sheepishly said, "No, I don't like football, but I like coming to the games." A big grin came across his face. He explained to me it was hard to promote football in a hockey city. If you don't know, Edmonton is home to the NHL hockey team, the Edmonton Oilers. Wayne Gretzky and Connor McDavid are our boys.

What Len did next was teach me about the game-day experience. He explained that the game was important, but just as important was what each person *experienced* during their visit to the stadium. It is a lesson every entrepreneur should take with them on every client interaction. Sometimes you only have one opportunity to make an impact so make it count; make it a game-day experience.

The next thing I thought we were going to chat about was my curiosity about how to build a performance-winning team culture. We started on that path and somehow got distracted by our mutual love of dogs. I knew Len and

Maureen were fostering a service dog named Oakley, a beautiful black Lab. Service dogs are trained from a very young age to support people with disabilities, mobility, and other challenges. When they first got Oakley, Len and Maureen remember thinking, "How is this smart, loving, mischievous black Lab ever going to be a service mobility dog?" Yet Oakley did great and served well.

Later, when I interviewed Len and Maureen for this book, I asked what it was like to let Oakley go. They know that the service dogs they help train are not their own. These special dogs are a gift to the world, and they are grateful to experience that gift, if only for a small moment in time. Maureen understood the purpose of the whole process, however Len cried all the way home after dropping Oakey off at his new home.

Len did eventually meet the person Oakley went to live with and when he saw them together, he understood. It came full circle, seeing how Oakley changed her life. They did everything together. Oakley especially helped build his person's confidence in *living* again. He helped with laundry and retrieving her phone and medication. Oakley's person was an actress, and he was even on stage with her at the Edmonton Citadel, as a cast member for one of her performances.

Len and Maureen are highly active in the community. Incredibly engaged, they volunteer for many events and organizations to support Edmonton's culture, business, sports, and non-profit groups. While attending a dinner event at the Expo Centre, Maureen left the table and did not come back for over 15 minutes. Len started to get worried. Upon her return, Maureen explained she had met a woman in the lobby who trained dogs to serve people with disabilities. She had a few service dogs with her, and Maureen met them. She was fascinated with the woman, named Maria. They decided to meet Maria together.

Len said that first meeting was like the universe brought them together in the perfect place at the perfect time. He and Maureen committed to getting to know Maria better. Together as a couple, Len and Maureen feel they have a shared purpose in life; they both love dogs and support the idea that dogs can serve a bigger purpose than just being a family member. They wanted to support Maria's work for many reasons. You see, within both of their families, they have members who have experienced disability challenges firsthand.

They loved what Maria was doing. She had impeccable credentials and was strongly committed to making a difference in the world by training dogs to support people with trauma, disability, and mental health challenges. That was enough for Maureen to fall in love with Maria's world. Maureen eventually left her successful marketing and advertising career to partner with Maria and, together, they founded Aspen Service Dogs.* Maureen believes the stars aligned to show her the way forward and do what she was meant to do.

Aspen began with 2 dogs and now they are training 70 dogs in Medicine Hat, Calgary, and Edmonton. Maureen shared, with a twinkle in her eye, that they train these beautiful dogs, and yet every day, the dogs teach her and Maria something.

---

*Aspen Service Dogs is an Alberta Government Qualified Service Dog Organization. Having met the requirements of the Alberta Training Standard, per the Service Dog Act of Alberta, Aspen Service Dogs prides itself on supplying highly trained, well-behaved canines that are able to perform a variety of tasks for their human partner. Aspen Service Dogs is one of only a handful of organizations approved to produce and train Service Dogs in Alberta.

Aspen is an incredible company. These dogs have big jobs; they are working dogs as well as family members and they support people in life and death situations. When that "Service Dog" jacket goes on, they have serious responsibilities. They need to be on high alert and act appropriately at all times. They go anywhere their human goes; Maria even took her service dog in training to jury duty.

Not all trainee dogs make it. Some are not cut out to serve in this way and that is okay. Each dog has its purpose. Those dogs that live to serve are chomping at the bit to work. Maureen says by the time they turn 2 years old, they want to move out of training and live their purpose. They *want* to work.

Together Len and Maureen have fostered 3 dogs and rescued one. Five years ago, they adopted Bella, a 9-year-old yappy Pomeranian and Jack Russell mix who stole their hearts. Bella was discarded by her owners. At the shelter, she was labeled as a "red zone" dog. In shelters, a red zone dog means the dog is unpredictable and could be aggressive and bite. The shelter put this 12-pound "red zone" dog in isolation and quarantine based on the information they had.

Maureen and Len both believe Bella was not a danger; she was simply scared for her life and did not have anyone to look after her or fight for her. We all need someone to fight for us, don't we? It turned out Bella was an amazing dog. She was only a 12-pound dog but taught them that you do not have to have big paws to create a big presence. Most days Bella would go to work at Aspen. When she walked in through those doors, she was the boss. They called her the General Manager and warned people not to mess with her.

Bella passed away almost a year ago and her presence is still felt by them every day. There is not one day that goes by that Maureen and Len don't talk about her. They know they saved Bella but feel Bella really saved them.

HOW DOGS MAKE US BETTER HUMANS

Len and Maureen have many stories founded on their love of dogs. They are grateful they have this shared love for the canine connection. You can tell they are a couple in love with life. They stand for doing good in the world and educating humanity on the incredible importance dogs can play in our lives. Whether your dog is a service dog, a family dog, or a working dog, there is one fact they believe is non-negotiable: dogs bring unconditional love to everything they do, and humans can learn a lot from that kind of love. Dogs can also help you change your career in the right circumstances LOL!

I WAS NOT A DOG PERSON

Story 6 - Being Present and Connected

"Dogs live in the present moment and when we are willing to be in the moment with them, life gets bigger, and life gets better."

— BEA BOHM-MEYER

I would be remiss if I didn't write about my dear friend and colleague, Linda Banister. Linda has recently retired after 30 years of owning her own business as a management consultant. Linda is a community leader, a savvy businesswoman, and a true entrepreneur. She owned her first firm for 8 years and her second firm for 22 years, selling the latter 3 years ago.

I think the slower pace of not running a business caught her off guard. Linda is a beautiful and kind person. She is also a triple-A personality with a passion to grow businesses and, more importantly, grow and nurture people. I have learned a lot from her, and she has been so generous in introducing me to the most extraordinary people. That is the type of person she is. Being a connector is important to her.

I would never in a million years have thought she would be included in my book. Up until 3 years ago, Linda had never even pet or held a dog. Not that she didn't like them or didn't think they were cute; Linda was raised in a family where her mom and dad just did not want pets in the house. Throughout her life, there was never any real exposure to dogs, much less interaction with them. And when she married her wonderful husband, she soon found out he was highly allergic to dogs. This was not a big deal since they were a dogless couple.

Fast forward to today. Linda has two successful grown children with amazing significant partners and three grand fur babies. I think she spends more time with those grand dogs than she does with her children. How does this happen? Well, a series of fortunate events.

First, it was her daughter Marina, who fell in love with a young man who had a 9-year-old Border Collie name Trigger. Trigger is gentle, kind, and a loving soul.

And then her son Taylor fell in love with Nicole, and together they got a Basenji puppy called Cleopatra. Linda was there for the adoption, and she describes the experience in such a loving and compassionate way. The family was in Palm Springs picking up the puppy together, which was so special. Linda compared the adoption to meeting a grand-child for the first time. As she described the first puppy greeting, I could feel her soul light up.

Linda was loving the two grand dogs when her daughter and future son-in-law decided to get another young Border Collie named Sully. Sully was to be a companion for Trig-ger. When Sully showed up, he was full of energy and very affectionate with a child-like wonder.

Linda explained to me that she didn't do all the things she was expected to do when she first retired; reading books, yoga, networking with people, taking long walks to find herself. Life was very different. Linda missed the energy of networking, constant social interaction, and what she missed the most was nurturing her team. You see, while Linda was building and growing the business, one of the most important roles she had was what she referred to as "spinning the plates." Her true role was to look after her team, watching them grow and helping them succeed wher-ever she could. She had 50 employees and every day she would try to understand what they needed to be successful. Each day she would spin the plate a little bit for each person, depending on what they needed at that time.

Her life today no longer consists of client meetings or networking opportunities bringing groups of companies together. Although, she does continue her board work and is passionate about mentoring start-up companies, particularly companies that are led by young women.

Linda's new schedule consists of picking up Cleopatra (Cleo for short) at 9:00 a.m. at her son Taylor's place. Many mornings there is also an opportunity to have a coffee with Taylor before Linda heads out to her downtown office just a block away. Linda takes Cleo for a walk, then heads back to the office where Cleo sits on her pillow throne with all her toys in front of the fireplace and takes a nap. Many times, Cleo just wants to play, and Linda will give her 100% of her attention.

Typically, in the afternoon, Linda will head over to Marina's house to pick up one of the dogs, whether it be Trigger or Sully, alternating days between them. They go for a walk and then Linda brings the dog back to the office, affectionately called The Puppy Palace.

As a nurturer, Linda gives the dogs exactly what they need. If they need to play, they will play. If they need to walk, they will walk. If they need to cuddle, they will cuddle. If they need a tummy rub or a total body massage, they will get that too. There are times when Linda could play for hours with Sully, throwing the toys up and down the stairs because that's what Sully wants.

HOW DOGS MAKE US BETTER HUMANS

Linda's first lesson she shared about her experience with these fur babies was that slowing down is not a bad thing.

She now understands that being present and honoring the moment is a joy for her. She appreciates when her mind stops racing and her soul becomes calm. We discussed how many people learn to be present from books, videos, and meditation. For her, the dogs are her teachers.

Her second lesson from these dogs is about connection. She spent 25 years working in her current office (a 113-year-old home in central Edmonton) and didn't know many of her neighbors. Walking these dogs has allowed her to connect to the people in the neighborhood and understand the tempo of the community. She is amazed at how dogs can bring people together.

Her third lesson is from observing the pure bliss the dogs get from simple activities and how that is an inspiration to appreciate life, especially the little things. She describes watching Cleo sit on her pillow "throne" in front of the fireplace staring at the fire – content, calm, and joyful.

Each night Linda reflects upon the day and asks herself if she did everything she could for those dogs and in turn, if she appreciated the joy in every moment. She is learning that simple pleasures are the greatest joys.

I want to thank Linda for sharing her story with us, as she's a private person. It is a great story of how dogs can weasel their way into our lives and our hearts when we are not looking.

SPORTS PSYCHOLOGY 101 - YOU TEACH WHAT YOU MOST NEED TO LEARN

Story 7 - Never Punish for the Sake of Learning

"Patience is when you understand that your dog is telling you something and you have the guts to listen."

— BEA BOHM-MEYER

I am so grateful to Maureen Mackay from Aspen Service Dogs in Edmonton, Alberta, and Len Rhodes, her significant other, who is also my friend. They introduced me to John Dunn. Maureen and Len suggested I give John a call. I didn't know what to expect but the introduction was well worth it for many reasons. John and I met for the first time over Zoom. The new trials and tribulations of the COVID-19 world eliminated an in-person meeting. I must share that John is a wonderful person with lots of stories, highly animated, has the best sense of humor, and possesses a passion for life. John is also Scottish, which probably explains a lot of what makes him a great story-teller. I loved every minute of our time together even if it was virtual. John shared a few very meaningful dog stories; however, I chose to write about only one. I will save the others for maybe, a second book.

John is a professor in the area of sport psychology at the University of Alberta. He teaches sport psychology classes at the undergraduate and graduate levels, is a researcher in sport psychology, and has an extensive background providing mental training and performance psychology support to elite athletes, members of the military, and members of Canadian law enforcement agencies. Interesting fact: he has provided support to Canadian athletes in a variety of sports at 3 separate Winter Olympic Games. In chatting, I could feel John's passion for what he does for athletes. John shared with me some tremendous lessons he has learned from dogs. Some of those lessons he has applied to his sports psychology teaching and practice.

John never grew up with dogs. He did mention a goldfish, but that seemed to be the extent of his childhood pet experience. His younger daughter Anna, on the other hand, had been drawn to dogs most of her life. Anna has a real zest for life, but throughout adolescence and into early adulthood, she faced some mental health challenges. According to John, her love for dogs has always been a type of personal therapy.

John explained that his next-door neighbor adopted a dog named Bruno shortly after her husband died. This would have been about 7 or 8 years ago. John goes on to describe how Anna just instantly latched on to this tiny little puppy and the Dunn house became Bruno's second home. It was the first time John experienced the power of a dog. Bruno brought Anna peace and joy, and to this day, the two are still 'joined at the hip.' John describes the relationship between Anna and Bruno as something incredible to observe and powerful to experience.

Fast forward to when Anna was doing her undergraduate degree at the University of Alberta. The school brought in therapy dogs around exam time to help the students with decreasing stress and pressure. It was here where Anna first met Maria Illes, co-owner and trainer from Aspen Service Dogs. Yes, the same Maria from Len's story. Anna enjoyed the interactions with the therapy dogs. She then bumped into Maria again at a local drug store a few months later, when it just so happened that Maria had another service-dog-in-training by her side. This meeting would change the lives of John's family forever.

Anna came home from the drug store and asked her dad if they could become an "Aspen dog foster and puppy-raiser." The dog would live with them until ready to go to a forever home as a service dog. Anna did all the research and presented her case. John and his wife Janice gave it some serious thought and also consulted with their other adult daughter, Kate. They did their own research, and eventually met Maria. John said they explored everything and did their due diligence. John also owned up to Maria, saying that he had no experience with dogs whatsoever other than through his dealings with military personnel who used dogs to assist in their work. He said to Maria, "I've been around military German Shepherds that are highly trained and highly specialized dogs, but these dogs are not pets." Shortly thereafter, John and his family met with Maria again and welcomed a 14-week-old yellow Labrador puppy named Bellamy into their home. I asked John to share the most significant lesson he experienced with Bellamy.

It was a morning when John needed to go to the university. He could not remember if it was for a class or a meeting. All he could remember was that he was late. As an Aspen dog raiser, you bring your dog with you wherever you go, so Bellamy was a frequent attendee in John's classes and meetings that were held on campus. This is a methodology used to socialize and familiarize the dog with everyday living and everyday experiences.

On this particular morning, Bellamy was outside enjoying the morning air. John went out to call her and apparently, she would not recall. He began to get frustrated and of course, Bellamy could sense his frustration. As John started to call louder, Bellamy started to move further and further away. John then began to raise his voice even louder, as it was getting seriously late. It became what seemed to be a stay-away game and things escalated. John's yard is big; therefore, Bellamy had a lot of room to move. As John yelled for Bellamy, Bellamy continued to run away. As he watched her, John had an epiphany: he needed to get his own emotions under wraps. He thought to himself in a very real moment, "Why would she come to me if I am upset with her?" John then took 10 seconds to pull it together. He went into the house, took a deep breath to calm down and got centered. Then he went back outside, gently sat at the bottom of the patio stairs, and just waited. There was no ask, no sound, and no demanding energy. There was just them; John on the step and Bellamy watching from a distance. Slowly, he took a treat out of his pocket and lovingly called her without a hint of frustration in his voice. He could see the smile on her face as she ran to him and showed him the trust he earned at that very moment. His older daughter Kate would remind him later that day, "Why would any *human* come to me if I raised my voice and sounded threatening?"

John said it was a marvelous moment for him. As a professional who applies performance psychology, he understood that we are all human and, in this circumstance, he had let his emotions get the best of him. His emotional brain was ruling his logical brain. He realized there is an importance of having patience with respect to changing behavior. You cannot just tell an athlete, a soldier, or a musician to perform. The same goes for your dog. You cannot just demand performance from anyone when they are learning new skills. It takes patience, trust, emotional control, and the ability to empathize with the person (or animal) you are working with. Maria said to John when they agreed to foster Bellamy, "You will never punish these dogs for the sake of learning." This is a lesson we can all learn.

While we were on Zoom, I could see Bellamy behind John lying on a bed. She looked so content, happy, and at peace. Each time John turned to look at her, his eyes lit up and his voice grew softer. It was a pure and unconscious demonstration of love. I could feel the love and connection they had with each other. As John talks about her, he also shares thoughts about the day Bellamy will go to her forever home; the day when she leaves for the home where she will live her purpose. That day will be a blessing and a hardship. He also shares that this time together has been a tremendous gift.

HOW DOGS MAKE US BETTER HUMANS

Maria's words are powerful: "You will never punish these dogs for the sake of learning."

Do we, as a human race, punish for the sake of learning? Is it a habit? Is it unconscious? What does this look like in our schools, universities, businesses, and sports teams? What does it look like in our communities? It is something to ponder. John has taken this one step further and included this learning in his sports psychology classes and practice when supporting students and coaching athletes. I will incorporate it wherever I can. How about you?

YOU CAN FIND HUMOR IN MOST THINGS, EVEN PORK TENDERLOIN

Story 8 - No Expectations

"The best things in life are unexpected. The best experiences in life have no expectations."

— BEA BOHM-MEYER

*G*et a dog, they said. Get a Lab, they said. It will be fun, they said.

My husband has a dear friend named Pierre. Well, I should say Pierre is a friend of our family. The friendship started many years ago and what connected Dan and Pierre initially were our two sons. Those two boys were passionate hockey players. The even deeper connection stemmed from both boys being goalies. Any goalie parent will tell you that being a goalie parent is certainly a different world.

In 2016 Pierre and his son Chase brought home a brand-new puppy; a chocolate Lab named Boomer. My husband always says when the Labs show up, the party begins. I know a lot of them and can confirm that as a fact.

A couple of years earlier, a devastating loss occurred for the family when Chase lost his mom, and Pierre lost his best friend and wife, to cancer. Her name was Kodi, and she was the heart of the family. The whole family was incredibly close and Kodi was the love of their lives. I never did get to meet her, but I felt her love and heart through this beautiful family. Dan, Pierre, and the boys had hockey in common, and I felt I had a little something in common with Kodi. We both knew the magic of dragonflies. Seemingly, dragonflies were a big part of her life and they showed up often for her and her family. Dragonflies have great meaning for me too.

I grew up with a sister who was 7 years older than me. Her name was Zsuzsa. She did not speak when she was young. The doctor said she needed someone to love. This is how I came to be. Zsuzsa was the most extraordinary sister. At times I felt like she raised me. When Zsuzsa graduated from high school she took me to Disneyland, just the two of us. When I had children, she loved them like her own.

When I was little, she told me that dragonflies were magical. "When you see one, it is to remind you that miracles are happening around us all the time."

Zsuzsa was taken from me too soon by ovarian cancer. There were days when she was in the hospital and there would be dragonflies resting on the outside of her window. It was like they were taking care of her. Soon after I lost Zsuzsa, a large dragonfly positioned itself on the front of my house for what seemed to be a very long time. Today I have dragonflies all around me. Whether I can see them or not, I know they are with me, connecting me more deeply to this world full of miracles. I understood why Kodi loved dragonflies. I understood why these mystical creatures kept showing up for both our families.

As you would imagine, when Kodi was gone, there was an emptiness in Pierre's home. And so it would be that in 2016 Pierre decided to get a dog. They had always wanted a dog and I'm sure Pierre thought that maybe this would help to heal their pain.

I don't know how to describe their dog, Boomer. He's almost indescribable. He is so handsome, exuberant, he loves life, mud, and his family. Did I mention he loves mud? My husband has the pleasure of walking Boomer as part of The Leash Team. He sees him almost every day. When he first started walking him, I was always scared because he was so rambunctious and full of piss and vinegar. I was afraid when I walked with them that he would knock me down with his excitable hugs. As years passed, he began to settle down and today, he is one of the leaders of our The Leash Team family of dogs.

I love walking with Boomer these days, in fact, I look forward to it. I feel he's always looking after me. When I walk with the team of pups, I intentionally remain at the back of the group. This way I get to see all the activity, all the joy, all the love and how the dogs explore and socialize. Can you tell I love it? This is good for my soul. During those walks, Boomer will socialize with the other dogs, but always comes back to see me. I feel he is checking on me and letting me know I am not alone.

There was one day when we were on a very steep bank, walking on a path overlooking the river. I lost my bearings and fell, rolling down the steep edge almost into the water. The other dogs were well in front of me and hadn't noticed but as I stopped sliding, I felt a wet breath on my neck. It was Boomer. I don't know where he came from because 30 seconds before, he was well in front of me. But now he was with me. It was the silliest thing, but I felt safe even though it was too steep to stand up. We sat there for a while. My husband had not noticed I was missing, but he did notice Boomer was missing and came to look for him. He found us both sitting in mud, quite content. Did I resent Dan for that? Looking for Boomer and not me? Nope. I love that he loves his dogs so much. It makes him even sexier to me.

There was one summer Chase and Pierre went off to hockey camp and asked if we could take care of Boomer. We were overjoyed of course. It was a weekend night, and I was watching Boomer sleep on one of the dog beds by the fireplace. It was very hot, so the fire wasn't on. The back door was open so the dogs could come and go as they pleased. We have a beautiful patio and an even more beautiful yard that mimics a small park. Our dogs were outside playing, while Boomer was inside sleeping. I decided to start dinner and took out a huge pork tenderloin from the refrigerator and put it on the counter. I turned around to take spices out of the spice cabinet. When I turned back, I found that the pork tenderloin had disappeared. I looked up and Boomer was no longer on the bed. I didn't see him anywhere until I stepped two feet into the living room and saw him looking at me with pure joy and the whole hunk of tenderloin in his mouth!

How could that be? How could he get from the bed to the kitchen within 10 seconds, let alone snafu our supper? The bugger! I yelled to Dan that Boomer had the tenderloin. Dan came running after him, chasing him like a bat out of hell. Dan was frustrated but I could tell he was laughing inside. As I watched Boomer running around the house and then into the yard while Dan continued chasing him, I couldn't stop laughing. It reminded me of an episode of *I Love Lucy*. (I know I am dating myself with that reference). It was as though Boomer thought this was a game. At one point Boomer stopped and Dan stopped, and they were 10 feet apart. I heard Dan saying "Nooooooo!" and in one big gulp, the pork tenderloin was gone. I was still laughing. All I could see was Boomer's face so full of joy and pride. I looked at Dan and said, "Perhaps we'll have shrimp tonight."

Boomer came into the lives of Pierre and Chase at the perfect time. He gave the family some reprieve from their broken hearts. I asked Pierre if they thought Boomer made them better people. His response was, "We got him in 2016 when Chase was 12. Chase always wanted a dog and when Kodi passed away, I figured it would be good for him to have a dog to care for. They grew up together and grew close. Boomer sleeps on Chase's bed whether he is there or not. Boomer has made all of us better people. For me, I had to practice patience around a young pup that wanted world domination. Boomer helps make Chase a better human in many ways. He taught him responsibility, and how to care for a pet. He taught him unconditional and never-ending love. He is always there in good times and bad. Maybe that is the lesson. Boomer was always there and together they could just *be*. No expectations. And because Chase was young when we got Boomer and there was no girlfriend yet, Chase had someone to play with." Pierre said with a laugh.

HOW DOGS MAKE US BETTER HUMANS

I love this story. Boomer was there to help take away the pain and show this family that love never ends. Love shows up in many ways in our lives. Boomer brought so much joy and love into their lives. Most importantly, Boomer was there for Pierre and Chase during the good times and the hard times, with no expectations. That is unconditional love and love without expectations is an incredible gift.

I ASKED THE UNIVERSE FOR YOU AND DID NOT EVEN KNOW IT

Story 9 - Healing

"Dogs are roles models for authentic servant leadership; love first, talk later."

— BEA BOHM-MEYER

The most extraordinary thing about owning a dog walking business is that you get to meet so many incredible dogs, and get to know people, families, couples, children, and grandchildren. In the case of The Leash Team, the company lives 4 Core Values: Trust, Love, Family, and Safety. As the team develops relationships with each client, the client is absorbed into our family. We are so privileged to be invited to client (family) BBQs, birthdays, Shabbat dinners, graduations, garden parties, etc. These relationships are gifts. These connections happen all because of the dogs. I know I could write a beautiful story about each of our clients' families. Maybe one day I will. For now, I will share a story about Onyx.

The Leash Team has a client, a jet-black Labrador Retriever named Onyx. He is handsome, goofy, and playful. Onyx is also pure joy, pure love, and is quite a handful. He is over a year now and starting to come into his own. I wanted to include him in this story because there is something powerful about putting stuff out to the universe, even if you do not know it.

I believe we all have a vibrational energy that talks to the world. I also think dogs can hear and interpret that energy loud and clear. How do I know this? I don't really, but is it not interesting that dogs show up in our lives when we need them the most? I also wonder what that says about me since I have a lot of dogs in my life. I guess I need a lot of help!

In 2019, Onyx's mom Catherine was taking care of her mom, who was slowly falling into the deep abyss of dementia. Catherine is such a beautiful and kind person. She was feeling deeply for her mom, but also feeling sadness for her family, knowing their connection to a loved one was slipping away. It is scary, frustrating, and unfair. Catherine lives with her young niece, River. They are very close and both wonderful people. Through many discussions and some research, they decided they wanted to adopt a service dog to assist both of them in healing past traumas. Or more specifically, a puppy that would grow up to be a service dog. Knowing a dog would be a big commitment, holding off on the adoption was the anticipated plan. Catherine was busy taking care of her mother and working. River was doing what young people should be doing, working extremely hard to design a good life. Unfortunately, Catherine's mother, through many unrelated and unfortunate circumstances, passed away unexpectedly. It was a difficult time for both River and Catherine. Life seemed to be standing still as they both grieved their loss.

Then shortly after her mother's passing, Catherine received a call about a black Lab who just had delivered 11 puppies. Curious and yet still with a heavy heart, Catherine and River decided to visit the puppies. They both wanted a Lab, and a black Lab was the bonus. As they visited the dogs, one midnight black puppy kept coming back to them. His name was "Sparkly Collar" because he had a sparkly collar. Well, you know how the adoption story ends. They felt that draw, that connection, and fell in love with Sparkly Collar.

They brought the puppy home and decided to re-name him Onyx. Onyx is a precious black gemstone. In many cultures, Onyx is known and used for its protective and healing powers. It is believed to absorb negative energy. It is also believed that Cleopatra wore black Onyx for its protective features. So, the story goes that when Cleopatra sensed negative energy, the crystal would vibrate, alerting the queen of potential danger. There is strength in the power of a name and Onyx brought that strength to this family.

Not to waste any time and like a good puppy mom, Catherine immediately invested in puppy training. Onyx did very well with crate training and basic obedience. However, it became quite clear that Onyx was a big bundle of energy and incredibly social. This fur baby loved life and had the energy to prove it. With so much enthusiasm, and a desire to connect, not only with humans but also with other dogs, Catherine sought out The Leash Team to help Onyx integrate into the world. This was how Dan and I met Onyx, Catherine, and River.

How often do you sit in gratitude because your passion has introduced you to other incredibly special human beings?

Well, Mr. Onyx brought Catherine and River to us, and The Leash Team was the perfect fit for Onyx, "The Protector." The off-leash group walks allowed Onyx to exercise and work off some energy, socialize with other pups, and learn appropriate dog behavior. He is a very curious puppy who loves friends and makes every walk fun and a unique experience. I will admit, sometimes his exuberance has the dog walkers either in a full out, bent over gut laugh, or patiently reigning him in from having just a little too much fun. It is extraordinary to watch this young male pup grow up.

The Leash Team hosts what we call Dog Adventure Days on the weekends. On one Adventure Day we celebrated Onyx's first birthday. Together with Catherine and River, we planned the birthday celebration as part of the day's event. They made little birthday cakes and frozen healthy treats for the dogs. So many treats! It was one of the best birthday parties I have ever hosted. We chose a special trail, we brought crazy doggy birthday hats and I swear the dogs knew we were celebrating Onyx.

Catherine wonders if her mom knew she was going to pass and sent "Sparkly Collar" to help heal their broken hearts. Catherine and River have had quite the journey in their lifetime, facing many challenges. Curiously, Onyx showed up when he did. Both spend a lot of time with Onyx. Dan and I get the privilege of sharing in most of his milestones. We get periodic notes and phone calls from Catherine. She shares what Onyx accomplishes and you can hear the joy, the love, and the pride. They should be proud. I can feel Onyx trying. I can see him learning. Best of all I get to experience Onyx's love.

River shared that Onyx brings them laughter when it is hard to find the positive. "He is very intuitive and will get into my face when times are tough. He demands cuddles and despite being 75 pounds, he becomes a lap dog." Even without specific training, Onyx is already helping Catherine and River by just being his intuitive self, sensing a change in them, and then helping them notice it too. Onyx is special. Like every other dog on this beautiful planet, each dog has a purpose and special gifts that they contribute to us. I know why Onyx showed up at the perfect time; Catherine and River needed him, and he needed them.

I may not know how it happens. I just know his presence is intentional. It supports the belief that everything happens for a reason. Well, kind of. I call it synchronicity. When your vibrational pull - your vibrational energy - is sending a message out into the world, and it is answered by a dog; that makes you lucky because that dog is just for you. A dog that will love you unconditionally, a dog that will teach you, a dog that will help you live a better life, a dog that will help you be a better human by ensuring you are connected to this world. It is not by chance. I know Catherine and River asked the universe specifically for Onyx, even if they did not know it. In this particular situation, I bet they even had a little help from Catherine's mom.

HOW DOGS MAKE US BETTER HUMANS

Do you think dogs show up in our lives when we need them the most? Have you ever thought about it? For Catherine and River, Onyx showed up for one reason: they needed him. They needed him to help the healing begin. Dogs can help us heal, encourage us to take one step forward and then another even if we do not want to. Dogs can help us get back to participating in the world even after great loss or trauma. For this Catherine and River are grateful.

A BUCKET LIST FOR BLOO

Story 10 - A love story

"There is a place in our hearts that belongs to them - the dogs that make us better humans."

— BEA BOHM-MEYER

*E*liza Kurdziel lives in Calgary, Alberta. She is passionate about life, is an adventurous soul, and a lover of dogs. She is also a pilot, which is pretty cool. About 15 years ago Eliza decided to move to the Turks and Caicos with her two dogs, Teak and Roxy. Excited about an adventure with her canine companions, they embarked on exploring the island and melting into the culture. Sadly, Teak died soon after they arrived, and Eliza was heartbroken. During this time, Eliza came to realize there were many stray dogs on the island and she wanted to do something about it.

Eliza heard about a lady named Jane, who had started an island dog rescue for the strays called Potcake Place. If you read the story of Bruce, which is story number 12 in this book, it is the very same place where Bruce was adopted from. The only reason Jane started Potcake Place was to alleviate pressure on the SPCA. The local SPCA was too full and wasn't accepting any more dogs and, unfortunately, some of the dogs were being euthanized. Jane's rescue was a no-kill operation. Eliza fell in love with what Jane was doing and ended up fostering over 500 dogs during her time on the island! She explained to me, "I could never foster fail. I was fine with giving the dogs back to go to adoption until I met Bloo."

Bloo was a stray found in front of a little island restaurant hut called the Conch Shack. I know the area well, as I had enjoyed a few refreshments and conch for lunch during my visit to the island a few years earlier. Someone found Bloo, who was six months old at the time and full of mange. Mange is a contagious and potentially deadly mite infestation. It was so bad, you could not even determine what color he was. The person who picked up Bloo brought him to the veterinarian who immediately called Jane, knowing she probably wouldn't say no to taking him. He said to her, "It's going to cost hundreds of dollars to heal this dog, and he is near death. He's so bad that he's going to be in quarantine for at least 2 months if he makes it." Jane said she could not take him, but of course ended up at his office an hour later to save this dog

After nursing him back to health, Bloo was finally ready for adoption and Jane posted his picture on the adoption site and sent a copy to Eliza. When Eliza saw the picture of this dog, a dog she had never met, she knew he was the dog for her. She found it strange that she had fostered over 100 dogs prior to seeing his picture, literally fostered the cutest puppies ever, and yet this "mange dog" with the soulful eyes was the dog that chose *her*, and she chose him. This was not going to be a foster; Bloo became family, even as Eliza continued to foster more pups.

Bloo was healthy for about 3 years before his health started to deteriorate. He was diagnosed with degenerative joint disease and needed surgery. The surgery required was not available on the island, so Eliza opted for the second-best option that was a similar surgery for smaller dogs.

Bloo was good for a few more years, then started to degenerate again. Eliza committed to fly to Miami and get the appropriate surgery. This time it was two surgeries, as both knees were afflicted. It was not the $5,000 bill she thought, it was a $12,000 bill she did not anticipate.

They lived on the island for another few years, before Eliza got a job in Thompson, Manitoba. She flew Bloo and her other dog, Roxy, from the warm sandy beaches of Turks and Caicos to the cold, great white north of Canada. They lived there for a while, then moved to Edmonton, and finally to

Calgary. By now, Bloo had lived in three countries and seven cities. Eliza's other dog, Roxy, lived to be 17 and a half years old and passed away while living in Calgary. It was a devastating loss for both Eliza and Bloo when Roxy passed.

As Bloo was getting older, Eliza kept reflecting on the role he played in her life. He was her constant companion, had an unconditional presence, and was an incredible support through her mom's cancer diagnosis and treatment. Eliza's mom is okay now, but it was one of the hardest years of her family's life. Bloo was also there through three of her major relationships and three big heartbreaks, numerous international moves, and always greeted her with his 'Potcake smile' and wagging tail when she came home.

Eliza knew Bloo had limited time on this earth. He was getting worse again and getting a bit older. Another surgery was required. In Calgary, it was the orthopaedic surgeon veterinarian who said there was a surgery he could do, but it would only potentially add a year to Bloo's life. The surgery cost $7,000 and the veterinarian said, "If this is my dog, I wouldn't do it."

Bloo got his final surgery and did amazing. He lived six more years after that surgery and every year, he would send his orthopaedic surgeon a Christmas card. The veterinarian loved it and was so happy Bloo was doing well.

There was so much unconditional love between them, and Eliza could not imagine life without Bloo. It was unbearable to even think about it. She did so much research and found out everything she could about arthritis degeneration and joint disease. She was also confident Bloo was not suffering. She could just tell he was happy and not in pain.

Fast forward to 2020, Bloo was not doing well again and the probability of putting him down was becoming a reality. Eliza's one last fight was to drive to an Edmonton clinic that was doing stem cell transplants and stem cell injections for dogs. The treatment was having amazing results in the USA and was new to Canada. Sadly, the treatment didn't work. Eliza realized there was nothing else she could do.

It was around this time Eliza started thinking, how could she celebrate Bloo's life before he crossed over the doggy rainbow? Then Eliza had the brilliant idea to create *Bloo's Bucket List*; a tribute to his life and love. It looked like this:

1. Bask in the sunshine all day, surrounded by an enchanted forest and listen to the birds sing

2. Be the guest of honor at a doggie dinner

3. Enjoy ice cream with the family (he barely walked at this point so Eliza built him a bike cart so she could take him for rides around the city)

4. Be an honorary fire station dog (the firefighters even made him turkey meatballs!)

5. Get a photoshoot by a professional photographer (Rachael Rodgers from @trailsandbears, Instagram influencer)

6. Meet someone famous (Bret Wilson)

7. Have a movie night with Mom and Polly

8. Eat McDonald's for the first time

9. Enjoy breakfast in bed (literally in Eliza's bed, with eggs and bacon)

10. Watch a sunset on a hilltop

11. Explore new places (visited 12 new parks)

12. Eat a gourmet meal cooked by a professional chef (AAA beef tenderloin)

13. Pass the 'cutest dog in the family' torch

14. Be a kid in a candy store (Eliza brought the pet store to his bed, with a selection of 10 dog bones/treats - he chose them all)

15. Date night with Mom

16. Donate food to an animal shelter

17. Have a birthday party to celebrate his 14 years and 5-month birthday

18. Try something new (arctic char and scallops)

19. Visit his favorite dog-friendly watering hole (Cold Garden) for the last time to say farewell to his doggie friends

20. Enjoy a family dinner night

21. Visit his favorite dog park for the last time

22. One last car cruise with mom (he loved car rides)

23 Get a one-hour massage

24. Listen to Mama read him his last bedtime story (Eliza wrote him a letter - it was a love story and Bloo and Eliza were the main characters)

25. His final bucket list item was the day after he passed - to collect donations for the rescue organization that rescued him, Potcake Place - they raised $1000 in his memory!!!

When I read this list, I cry for each experience and each celebration. The care, love, and compassion that honors Bloo's life are so real, authentic, and heartfelt. By the end of Bloo's life, Eliza spent more than $20,000 on surgeries and therapies to help him live an extraordinary life despite his early age bone disease. Yet, it was not the surgeries and treatment that made his life extraordinary, it was their love for each other; a love without boundaries or expectation, a love that nurtured their souls and fed their hearts.

As time progressed the daily treatments were not working. The pills Bloo took were wearing off and he was getting a little bit sleepier and more tired each day. He didn't want to go outside for as long, and eventually she knew she had to let him go. Eliza felt Bloo was telling her he was ready. He passed on June 9th, a devastating day for her.

After Bloo's passing, Eliza's current dog, Polly (a dog she got specially to be Bloo's companion in his final stages of life), carried bits of food to Bloo's bed. Although Bloo and Polly slept on that bed together, Polly never slept on that bed again. Before Bloo passed, Eliza asked him to send four-leaf clovers and feathers. In the first year he was gone, she found 37 four-leaf clovers, 5 five-leaf clovers and many beautiful feathers! There was a time Eliza did not want to go to her mom's house because one of Bloo's favorite places to nap was the front porch. The day she chose to help her mom unpack groceries was the day she found a beautiful feather on the porch, telling her that he was happy somewhere over that beautiful rainbow bridge.

After Bloo's passing, Eliza shared a personal message on Facebook. Here is an excerpt:

But finally, all great things come to an end and in the past week he was clearly telling me his time on this earthy plane must come to an end, his job was complete. He was ready to go. With all the love, courage, kindness, and respect I could muster, I let him go to that far away place everyone hopes is real.

His last heartbeat thumped at home, on his bed covered in flowers, surrounded by his friends and family. I was laying beside him, holding his paw, kissing his head, whispering our love story's greatest moments in his big floppy ears.

Even the saddest of days can be the most profound, beautiful, and powerful. I cannot help but to acknowledge that the reason for my immeasurable, gut wrenching, heart shattering pain is because of a lifetime of memories made, a decade and a half of love shared with this beautiful legend of a dog. That is enough to be grateful for the pain and bear its sadness.

No more daily pill popping, Bloo. You no longer need me, your walking aid, or even your fun bike cart. You can break free from your crippled legs and run and play in those endless green fields over the rainbow.

Your life was my greatest love story...and it'll never end. I will forever keep and cherish our eternal bond. There was always something very special about you. Be like Bloo, my friends. Strong, yet soft. Brave, yet goofy....and always persevere.

Rest easy my Disney Dog. Potcake smiles forever.

HOW DOGS MAKE US BETTER HUMANS

Bloo taught Eliza how to love unconditionally and without any expectations in return. She shares, "These days it's easier to connect deeply with others when you give them your time, loyalty, vulnerability, and open heart. Having a pet is like showcasing all the beautiful traits that humans naturally embody, but sometimes hide away so that we do not get hurt. Having Bloo in my life has graciously taught me that."

ARE EIGHT EMERGENCY CONTACT NUMBERS ENOUGH?

Story 11 - Family comes in all shapes and sizes

"Dogs can be many things to many people. For me, dogs will always be family."

— BEA BOHM-MEYER

J met Lori and Rick Dykhuizen in 2017. They are such a nice couple with an adventurous spirit, incredibly kind-hearted, thoughtful, and joyful. Dan and I laugh a lot when we are around them. Lori and Rick are passionate about spending meaningful time with family and friends. If you ever needed anything, they would be the first to offer support. They are also committed to building community. Whenever possible they shop locally and will remind you to do the same. I love that about them. You also might have already guessed, both of them are crazy about dogs. If Rick and Lori are not visiting with family, walking their dog, or cooking a wonderful meal for friends, they are most likely traveling. One of their favorite places to get away from it all is a little island called Maui. Keep this in mind when you learn the name of their dog.

Lori and Rick married late in life. They both felt it was too late to have children, human children that is! Wanting to grow their family, they decided to bring a fur baby into their lives. Rick has some pretty severe allergies, so researching different breeds was a priority. The Labradoodle breed seemed to be a perfect fit, with a gentle temperament and being hypoallergenic. Once the decision was made on the type of dog, there was no turning back.

Before ever meeting their future family addition, Rick and Lori chatted about what they would name their dog. One night while in Maui they picked up pizza and beer and brought the meal back to the villa they were staying in. After supper, Rick said, "If our puppy is a girl, I think she should have a Hawaiian name." Lori went to grab her beer and saw it was a *Kona Longboard* and said "What about Kona?" Rick quickly responded, "I love it! How did you come up with that name?" Lori turned her beer around to him and said "Beer." They quickly researched the name. Kona meant "lady" and "world rule." The decision was made.

In 2015 they found a trusted breeder and eventually arranged to meet the newest litter of puppies. The puppies were about 5 weeks old and all cute as can be. Yet, both

Lori and Rick noticed one pup that stood out. This little fur ball had a whole lot of personality and sass, and so it was meant to be. Although they chose Kona on that day, Lori believes that in reality, it was Kona who chose them. And yes, they did name her Kona.

Lori described Kona as "incredibly loving, affectionate, loves people probably more than dogs, and most importantly, everyone who meets Kona loves her a ton in return. She's more human than a Doodle. "

When Rick and Lori decided to bring Kona into their lives, they also committed to giving her the very best life possible. They were all in. Both worked their schedules around Kona's needs. To this day, they have never left Kona at home for longer than 4-5 hours.

When going out together, whether it's visiting with family or friends, a walk, a drive, or going on vacation, it is always an adventure all three will enjoy. Weekends are the most favorite days. Lori shares, "Waking up with Kona between us is THE BEST! I love listening to her sighs and snores and love the feel of her breath on my skin. I can't count the number of times that I've gotten up late because I wanted to savor the feeling of her beside me." Rick, Lori and Kona generally sleep in on the weekends, have breakfast (Kona gets a special breakfast), go for long walks, enjoy afternoon naps, and spend the evenings either cheering on the Edmonton Oilers hockey team in the winter, or outside in the gazebo during the summer. Most importantly, the three of them are together.

When they first brought Kona home, Rick owned an insurance adjusting company and Lori worked in hospital administration (she still does). Life was busy and they came to realize Kona could benefit from some stimulation, exercise, and socialization outside of the family. In doing research, can you guess what happened? Yep, you guessed it. They hired The Leash Team, hoping Kona would make new friends and have a whole new experience being with dogs instead of spending most of her time with humans. It was a joyful and interesting experience. Initially, Kona loved being with the people more than the dogs. She walked alongside whoever the dog walker was that day. Instead of playing with the dogs, she watched all the dogs play in front of her. At times it felt like Kona was helping to walk the dogs rather than being a dog. Did she think she was human?

The day came when Lori and Rick decided to plan another trip to Maui. They asked Dan and me if we could take care of Kona while they were gone. We were thrilled and honored, particularly because we knew how over-protective they were of their little fur baby. Little did we know we would first have to pass "the test."

A month before their trip, Lori and Rick planned a date night. There was a hockey game that night. Dinner and a game were the perfect opportunities to leave Kona with us. Part of the plan was to have Kona sleep over. We were excited. When they dropped Kona off, we were provided with the dog boarding information sheet we normally request for overnight visits. It was filled out with precise detail. They also provided us with an additional 2-page laminated document outlining more personal doggy information and special instructions. They felt the extra information would be helpful to ensure Kona did not miss them as much as they thought she would. I get it. It was Kona's first sleepover.

The additional information included 8 emergency phones numbers. It seemed we had access to their entire family contact list. When I share this story with others it always makes me smile. We were also provided with detailed instructions on how Kona likes to sleep, play, and do her business, as well as a list of all the snacks she gets throughout the day. Options of raw and cooked carrots, strawberries, watermelon, cheese, and dog treats, to name a few, are given after walks, doing her business, naps, and playtime. Her favorite foods are enjoyed at dessert and bedtime. These snacks usually consist of berries or frozen bananas and peanut butter. Lori, who is always very thoughtful, packed additional treats for all of the dogs that would be staying with us during Kona's sleepover. She does this every time Kona visits. When I read the treat list, I felt bad. I don't think I fed my children this well while they were growing up! It was an endearing list and we loved her for it. We still have that list and every time I look at it, I feel so much love, and it makes me hungry for frozen bananas and peanut butter.

While Lori and Rick were at the hockey game, we were enjoying Kona. I think we only had six phone calls from Lori wanting to make sure Kona was comfortable. I did not tell her Kona was more than comfortable hanging out with me, sitting in my chair, watching the game on TV. Kona loved being with us. She did not play with our dogs back then. She did, however, play with us humans. It was then that I started to realize Kona felt more human "than dog" and it made total sense. Kona, for most of her formative years, only had Rick and Lori. Those three did everything together. They were a family unit. Kona was two years old when she started to socialize with other dogs. It wasn't that she did not like other dogs. She loved our dogs, she just preferred to hang with us humans.

When Rick and Lori did eventually go to Maui, we were allowed to take care of Kona. Yes, we passed the test!!!!! During this first long stay with us, Kona did act more human than dog. I remember each night I would say good-night to my dogs and jump into bed. Right after that, Kona sniffed both my dogs and jumped into bed with me. One night I asked Dan, "Do you think she is saying good night to our dogs?" We both giggled.

To this day, we tease Lori and Rick about the detailed instructions they left for us. Although it was only 2 additional laminated pages of detailed information, we tease them that it reads like a short story. We also continue to tease them about how they spoil their little fur baby. I guess I should be careful not to tease too much. I did invite Kona over one day to have a girl's day with me. We ate our favorite foods, went for a walk, watched a girly movie, did facials, and I gave her a massage.

Kona has come a long way from the dog that would only walk beside a human and watch the other dogs play. Today she tries to integrate more with the dogs, on her terms. She has an adorable and awkward play request. She bows to the other dogs and barks. It seems like she is asking them to play. She will play for a brief time, then resume her position beside the dog walker. Kona does play with my dog, Eddie. There is a special bond between them. Girl Power!!

This year Lori and Rick toyed with the idea of getting a second dog to be with Kona. After much discussion, they're still undecided if it's the right path because Kona was not socialized at an early age. Her comfort level is more with humans and her mom and dad than it is with dogs.

When you see this family together, there is no doubt the love and loyalty Kona exhibits for Rick and Lori comes with a pure heart and is unconditional. Kona and Lori have a thing where they take turns kissing each other on the nose; Kona understands "my turn" and "your turn" – it's the sweetest thing to watch. ♥ Lori shares, "So often, we'll find Kona staring at us with her beautiful brown eyes and it's so intense that it reaches the depths of our souls and we know without a doubt that the love we have for each other is deep and real." Kona makes them laugh every day and brings much happiness into their lives & home. They believe, because of Kona, they have met many wonderful people and without Kona, they would have missed out on these opportunities of connection, including connecting with us - the Bohm-Meyer family. Kona also helps them keep healthy by getting them outdoors, doing things whether they want to or not.

Will Kona get a sister or brother? For now, being exposed to dogs on the group walks is the right amount of balance for Kona to be a dog and to let her think she is human.

HOW DOGS MAKE US BETTER HUMANS

Lori and Rick share that Kona has taught them many life lessons. "Never in a million years did we know just how much WE would change the day we brought Kona into our lives and home."

Kona taught them the meaning of unwavering loyalty, unconditional love, patience, living in the moment, taking time to smell … everything. Kona knows how to comfort them and make them smile on the hardest days. Most importantly, Kona taught Lori and Rick that love and family come in many different shapes, sizes and experiences. These three are a family unit as much as any family I know. They live, love, share in the joy, comfort in sorrow, and are there for each other always. I say, where there is this kind of love, and loyalty there is family, and that is a beautiful way to live life.

EXTRA SPECIAL STORIES BY GUEST CONTRIBUTORS

HIBO AND ME

Story 12 - Don't Worry, Be Happy

---

*"With challenge comes growth if you are open to it.
Dogs have a way to help us be open to it."*

— BEA BOHM-MEYER

WRITTEN BY PHYLLIS BRIGHT

PHYLLIS IS AN EXTRAORDINARY BUSINESSWOMAN IN OUR COMMUNITY. SHE HAS OWNED AND OPERATED THE FLAG SHOP FOR 26 YEARS. SHE IS A MOM AND GRANDMOTHER (BOBBI) TO THREE AMAZING GRANDCHILDREN. WE LIKE TO CALL HER BOSS LADY AND DOG MOM WITH A BIG HEART.

*A*ll my life I've always had dogs. When I was growing up, as a young adult living on my own, and then with my family. But there came a time when I was alone – my last dog had passed a year earlier, and I struggled with getting another dog. I was in my 60s, with mobility problems. I started looking at rescue sites to see what I could find.

I found a few dogs that looked promising, but nothing worked out. Then I was speaking to an acquaintance in Vancouver who worked with a rescue dog organization in Taiwan. Until recently, stray dogs in that country were taken to kill shelters. Several rescue organizations were working hard to get as many dogs out as possible. She introduced me to a lady who asked a million questions and then said, "I have the dog for you. I'll send a picture." The picture was a headshot of a sleek black head with the most wonderful ears I have ever seen. Something *called* to me. I couldn't believe that a picture could pull at my heartstrings like that. So, I asked for more information.

The dog in the photo was a Formosan Mountain Dog (FMD). He had been fostered for a year and a half. Because he had a black head and 3 legs, he was considered undesirable. He had lost his leg when he was hit by a car while running on the highway in Taiwan. After a couple of surgeries, they had to amputate his hind leg, leaving him with 3 legs and a plate in his good hip. I felt that I *had* to adopt him. I got several videos of his life in Taiwan, and I just fell in love with him more and more. There happened to be a flight leaving Taiwan in a few days, with a volunteer and 5 dogs.

What do I do? Do I bring a dog over that I have never met? My kids thought I was nuts and weren't really in favour of the whole situation. But the more I saw of him and the more I thought about it, the more I wanted him.

He arrived in Vancouver in August of 2017. I flew there to pick him up. He was a bit standoffish when he came off the plane, which was to be expected. I hadn't done any research into his breed of dogs, which proved to be a good thing – I am not sure I would have proceeded had I done that!

For the first 2 weeks, I couldn't touch Hibo. As I did not speak Taiwanese, I kept his name because that was the only word he knew and at least it would be familiar. He would let others put his leash or collar on but wouldn't come near me. I thought it was because I told him I was his mom. He was probably thinking, "You say you are, but I'm not going to get too close until I know for sure."

FMDs are by nature skittish, anxious, strong-willed, and incredibly loyal to one person. He was all those things. After lots of patience on both our parts, he has become a calm, confident, and is still a strong-willed boy who is very loyal to me. He is not affectionate in the Labrador sense of the breed. He is not a cuddler or a kisser (except to a select few). I know he would fight to the death to protect me. He seems to know when I need a bit of extra attention. Even if I cry during a sad movie, he gets concerned and I must reassure him that all is good. During the pandemic, he was my lifeline to communication.

Hibo has an uncanny ability to know who truly loves him and who tolerates him. Hibo has a dog walking team (The Leash Team) who loves his quirks and individuality. Although I am sure it is sometimes frustrating, they work with him, and he feels happy and loved. I see in the pictures and stories they share of his joyful adventures.

I have become one of "those" dog moms. I know I spoil him, but I try and do it in a healthy way. He starts every day with a latte – hemp milk and Green Mush, which is a green supplement. He has a dog food breakfast. For dinner, I cook his food. He has come to look forward to that. He doesn't care what I make – if it comes out of a pot on the stove, it must be good.

Because of his accident, he has some minor spinal issues, and he has a plate in his good hind leg. So, he has sessions in laser treatment and acupuncture. He doesn't mind those, but he doesn't like the massage, so we don't stress him by doing them. He also has his own chiropractor that he sees monthly. I do these things so that as he ages, he will be comfortable. Even though he only has 3 legs, his dog walker tells me that he runs almost as fast as the other dogs. In the summer, he can be found swimming in the river whenever possible. I love that he does not know he is different, or just doesn't care. He has also been known to scoot away to find a spot to roll in the mud or other disgusting things, but he can always be found, as he wears a GPS tracking device.

I have been asked what Hibo means to me. To say "everything" is cliche and true at the same time. I often plan my life around what is best for him. I try not to go out in the evening if I have been at work all day. Even though he has been out for an hour or 2 on his walk, he doesn't like for me to leave him twice in one day. I do curb-side grocery pickups on Saturday mornings, so he can come with me. He knows when it is Saturday and heaven help me if I go out without him! I get a lot of whining and evil eye looks. As with many dogs, he has a clock in his head and stomach. If I am home during the day, he starts to whine at 3pm – it is time for an apple. At 5pm he whines for dinner. I seldom set my alarm clock in the morning – we are up at 6am, 7 days a week.

About a year after I brought Hibo home, I had him "read" by an intuitive person. I know that many people think it is hogwash, but I am open to many things. I asked her to find out if he did love me, why he whined in the car – did he get car sick? – and anything else he chose to tell her. Yes, he did love me (whew), but would I please stop calling him baby, and he whined in the car because he was excited to go on adventures. He was happy and I was relieved.

Hibo isn't spoiled at all. At least not any more than any other beloved pet. In the winter, he does like to have the heated seats on, and at least one window open. Of course, I comply.

Dogs provide their humans with a lot of different things. They show us love in different ways and communicate with us in various manners. Hibo lets me know what he wants, and he tries to tell me what he can do for me. He answers when I ask him a question, and through nonverbal communication tells me when he is not happy with me. He gives me a sense of security and peace.

I look at what he has been through in his short life – a traumatic accident, 2 different homes on 2 different continents; the second one speaks a strange language, although Siri was a big help in translating. He has been through all kinds of weird treatments, including needles sticking into him. But if I am with him, I know he will feel that all will be ok, and he doesn't have to worry. That is how I feel as well. People tell me that he is lucky that I adopted him. I feel that I am the lucky one.

HOW DOGS MAKE US BETTER HUMANS

Hibo has made me understand the importance of patience. Being a normally impatient person, it was difficult for me to buy into the concept.

He has made me understand that there is no such thing as a special needs dog. Although Hibo has 3 legs instead of 4, he doesn't understand that he is deficient in any way. He is unique and he is whole. He has taught me to downplay my own problems. Perhaps he reminded me that I am unique, and I am whole. There is an unconditional love that bonds us. I plan my life around him, not because I have to, it is because I want to. He has also kept me active in a way. His care is expensive, so he has kept me working long after the age that most people retire. Maybe that is not so bad either.

BRUCE HAS ITS PRIVILEGES

Story 13 - Privilege

"To be loved by a dog is a privilege. To love a dog is an honor."

— BEA BOHM-MEYER

WRITTEN BY JANICE MEYER

JANICE IS MY AMAZING SISTER-IN-LAW AND IS MARRIED TO MY HUSBAND'S BROTHER, JAK. TOGETHER THEY HAVE 2 BEAUTIFUL DAUGHTERS, SYDNEY, AND KAMRYN. THE FAMILY LIVES IN BRITISH COLUMBIA AND OWNS MEYER FAMILY VINEYARDS. THE WINES ARE HIGHLY RECOGNIZED, AND THEIR CHARDONNAY IS MY ABSOLUTE FAVORITE AND A MUST TO EXPERIENCE.

*B*ruce is a Potcake. We adopted him as a puppy when we lived in the Turks and Caicos Islands. Potcakes are the feral dog of the Bahamas and the Turks and Caicos Islands. They are called Potcakes because the locals used to cook in a big pot over the fire and all the food would stick (or cake) to the bottom of the pot. When they finished eating, the pots would be moved into the bush where all the wild dogs would eat; hence they are called Potcakes.

They are a lovely mixed breed and typically a medium-to-large type of dog. Their personalities are sweet and kind. There is a great organization called Potcake Place (www.potcakeplace.com), a large rescue on the island. Bea and Dan were visiting when our family adopted this wee Potcake. And here begins the story of Bruce.

He is called Bruce because the dog rescuers found him as a little puppy in the bush with a dirty white tank top ala Bruce Willis from the Die Hard movies and the name just stuck. We did not want to change it. We lived on the island for 4 years and Bruce was a big part of our family. One of my favorite stories of living there was when we took our boat over to a small island called Iguana Key. My parents were with us at the time and this island was uninhabited except for all the large iguanas. Bruce quickly ran into the bush and came running out with a large iguana in his mouth. Bruce was full-grown by that time and this iguana was so big that its tail was dragging in the sand, and it had claws about 2 or 3 inches long! My mom, who was not a great swimmer, quickly turned around and headed into the ocean as to not come close to this iguana! Iguana 0 - Bruce 1.

My husband Jak had to go and fight Bruce to open his jaws and let the iguana go. He promptly scurried back into the bush. Not 5 minutes later, Bruce was back in the bush, and we heard a yelp, and he came out - a little sheepishly - with a big scratch across his nose. Iguana 1 - Bruce 1. We were happy to leave it as a tie.

One year, we had come home to Canada for 3 months in the summer. We left Bruce with our house sitters there in the Turks and Caicos. Our house was on a canal and Bruce got in the habit of jumping the fence and swimming across the canal to a neighbor's house. We did not know these folks, nor did we know he visited them. Apparently, he visited often. However, once we were back on the island, Jak was golfing one day and mentioned Bruce. A fellow he was golfing with quickly got on the phone and said "Hey honey, guess who I'm golfing with? Bruce's dad!"

We soon found out these dear folks across the canal were giving Bruce steak for dinner. No wonder he was so committed to swimming across the canal to get his steak. How neighborly of him to visit most days! The neighbors never did invite us over for a steak. I wonder if we should take that personally LOL.

Another great memory while living in the Turks and Caicos was walking a long stretch of beach, which we often did with Bruce. It was interesting because part of this stretch was a nudist beach. One day, Bruce takes off at a dead run. He ends up visiting this couple who seem quite taken by him. They are giving him all sorts of hugs, belly scratches, and loving him like he was their dog. The craziest thing of all is that they were calling him by name. We slowly came to learn that our little Bruce was quite famous on the island. He was a bit of a wanderer those days. We thought we built a high enough fence, but he just jumped over it. To finish up the nudist story, there we were, having a lovely and long conversation about Bruce with a friendly and completely naked couple! You know how your children have friends and they introduce you to their parents? Bruce kind of did the same thing, although it never really mattered to him if they had clothes on or not.

When we loaded up everything to come back to Canada, we had to put Bruce in a crate. He had to ride as cargo in the plane. At the airport, he was so excited and nervous. We felt the same. We took him for many walks before we got on the plane and our flight was from Provo to Dallas, approximately 6 hours. We arrived in Dallas and rushed to get Bruce. We took him out of the crate and then for a long walk while we waited for our luggage. You would think he would have had to do his business by then, but he did not go. We got to the hotel where we were staying for one night and took him for another long walk, and he still did not go. We took him back up to our room and went for dinner. Before bed we took him for another long walk. He was so excited, but he still did not pee. So, we went to bed because we had to catch an early morning flight. In the morning, we begin to panic because he had not gone pee for close to 24 hours! Just before we boarded the shuttle to the airport for another 5-hour flight, Bruce finally lifts his leg and has the longest pee known to man. It probably went on for 5 minutes! We were laughing our heads off. What the heck was that all about anyway?

Back home in Canada, Bruce continued his wandering ways. We landed in British Columbia and eventually ended up farming. Well, not what normal people would call farming. We started a very special Vineyard called Meyer Family Vineyard. Wherever we lived, Bruce was well known. He is a very friendly dog and had many adventures. Before we moved to the vineyard, he went on his group walks at his doggy daycare. He was the dog who chased a bear, challenged a porcupine, and lost, and grabbed a pheasant out of the bush. He was infamous *and* famous!

He became single-minded when chasing his prey. One day on a hike, he chased a marmot right off a cliff! We were expecting the worst, but thankfully it was only about a 15 ft drop and he was just bruised. He has also chased many a deer and has been chased and trampled by a few angry mama deer.

Bruce has spent most of his long life here at the winery with 20 acres of vineyard to roam. He is the chief dog around this place and has many canine friends. What an amazing life for a dog. He's now almost 15 years old. He has slowed down quite a bit. No more chasing marmots, rabbits, pheasants, deer, or iguanas. He's quite content to spend most of his days sleeping in the sun, on the porch, by the vines, and with us in the house. He came into our lives when our girls were so young, and they do not know a life without him. Being so far away from family and friends can be hard. Bruce was one of the bonds that made the island normal, fun, loving, and mischievous. The bond between our family and Bruce is special and so strong. He is simply one of us. He may be canine, and we may be human, but we are family.

The bond between my husband Jak and Bruce is, I would not say strongest, but more deeply connected. Bruce is always on the lookout for Jak, watching his every move. He is happiest by Jak's side. They are two peas in a pod walking the vineyard. There are few words exchanged between them, yet I feel they communicate better with each other than most human beings.

HOW DOGS MAKE US BETTER HUMANS

We have learned a lot from Bruce. Of course, when we think of him, love comes to mind but so does privilege. It has been an incredible privilege having Bruce as part of our family, a privilege we will never take for granted and a privilege we will also remember. We don't know what the world will look like without Bruce, and we do not want to think about it. Whatever it looks like, we will always feel privileged to be loved by him. It reminds me that many people in our lives make an impact on us. We should never forget the privilege of connections we make and the relationships we form. It is a privilege.

Bruce passed away in June 2021. He is dearly missed and dearly loved. Rest in peace, Bruce.

HOW MUCH IS THAT DOGGIE IN THE WINDOW?

Story 14 - Selflessness

"When you take a chance on a dog, you give the world another reason to love you, because a dog is your whole world."

— BEA BOHM-MEYER

WRITTEN BY PHOEBE PABLO

PHOEBE IS ONE OF MY DAUGHTER'S BEST FRIENDS, A LONG-TIME FAMILY FRIEND, AND NOW A FULL-TIME EMPLOYEE OF THE LEASH TEAM. SHE IS CERTIFIED IN DOG BEHAVIOUR AND TRAINING METHODOLOGY (DBTM), HAS COMPLETED AN INTENSIVE DOG WALKING CERTIFICATION PROGRAM, AND IS CERTIFIED IN PET FIRST AID AND CPR. SHE HAS HER BUSINESS ADMINISTRATION CERTIFICATE AND HAS PLAYED A VITAL ROLE IN BOTH RETAIL AND HOSPITALITY LEADERSHIP.

$\mathcal{T}$he year is 2005 and I'm 10 years old. My sister was working at the mall. Since she was only 16 at the time, my family and I would usually go to the mall early to pick her up. We would often window shop to pass the time while we waited for her. The entrance we parked our car was positioned perfectly because we had to pass by a pet store. My dad and I would always look at all the animals together. From an early age, it was clear my dad and I were similar in many ways. I loved to shadow him. I grew to be creative like him. He would paint something, and I loved to try and replicate it. He started to learn how to use "new" animation technology (vcad) and I would do voiceovers and make little movies. I was a lover of animals because of him. He knew so much about animals, and in so much detail, that we call him Mr. National Geographic. He would constantly quiz us on animal information as if it were a life skill.

One day my dad and I passed the pet store and saw two beautiful Corgi pups in the display window. This was 15 years ago when animals could be bought at shopping malls. We played with the pups through the glass until my sister met up with us and we went on our way. To be honest, there was no love at first sight. Angels did not sing to us. Lightning did not strike.

We passed by the store again, and again, and again each day. We had visited one particular pup about 3 or 4 times, and we could see her growing each day. Each time we saw her, we fell a little more in love with the "doggie in the window." As kids of course, we had asked if we could have a dog, and the answer was no. We knew the first "no" was always final, or so we thought.

We saw the pup again and somehow, no one had claimed her. My mom who, by the way, is afraid of dogs, told me years later that a little voice told her, "Just because you didn't have a pet growing up, doesn't mean you should deny your children of the experience." The next bit is very fuzzy for me. There were calls made to the pet store, to the vet, to a puppy training school, and lastly to my dad at work. As you have probably guessed by now, we went from how much is that doggie in the window to that doggie is now in our house.

It was sort of like one moment it was a hard no, and then suddenly, we're bringing home a puppy. Let's be clear. We had no idea what we were doing, but lo-and-behold, as a family we were in it together. We promised to band together, to help train her and love her unconditionally. We read about the breed. We bought books to help us navigate puppyhood. We, as a family, were excited to have a pet, a companion, and a fur ball to be in our lives for the next 10-15 years. She was ours and we were hers. There is nothing like it. There were so many lessons during these years and I would like to share three of them with you.

LESSON 1

This was one of the most important lessons. My mom's selflessness provided us with an opportunity to experience life in the most loving way. As dogs always put hoomans first, my mom always put us first. She swallowed her fear of dogs so we as a family, could love unconditionally. In the end, it was Ginger (we named her Ginger) *and my mom* who showed us unconditional love. For that, I will be forever grateful.

Our life with Ginger was quite normal. She was a good puppy, although she had her moments. The thing about Ginger is that she was more like a cat than a dog. We would put her in her pen that stood 5 feet tall and when we came home, the dog would be roaming loose in the house. How? Not sure. When she took her naps, she would sleep on the chairs of the dining room table while they were tucked in. To this day we never knew how she possibly could have gotten herself to fit in such a small space. She was a sweet dog and very sassy. She did not like the outdoors and she had no interest in meeting other dogs. We loved her still for her cat-like tendencies and personality. We knew she kind of liked her space, so we gave it to her.

Fast forward about a decade or so. Ginger started showing signs of aging. She would move slower and be less inter-ested in just about anything. Her health wasn't declining at an alarming rate, but it was showing her age. She started to be a little more dependent and a little less defiant. Each day at 6:30 pm on the dot, Ginger began a strange ritual. She would pick herself up and lay by the front door and whine. At first, we weren't sure why, but it became clear as time went on. Ginger was waiting for my dad. My sister was older, my brother was older, I was older, and for Ginger, that meant change. Life was busy and schedules were inconsistent. The one thing Ginger could rely on was my dad. He arrived home at 6:30 pm every evening. She would lay by the door, wait for his arrival, and greet him with her open heart. She got her well-deserved pets and tickles and then could go back to wherever she liked to hide. This was her ritual. She was loyal to the rhythm of the day. I never did ask my dad what it meant to him, but in my heart, I know that love and that kind of loyalty is who we are as a family. It is how we show up for each other as a family.

LESSON 2

Sticking to a schedule can settle the mind. Relying on a schedule and daily rituals lessens chaos. When you build rituals into your life, there is less time and space for worry. Boundaries create the feeling of safety and I learned that from Ginger. No matter what the day held, or who showed up when, her favorite part of the day was greeting my dad. Since it was important to her, she built it into her day and stuck to it. She made time for what she loved. That is a freaking powerful lesson.

The dog in the window had made it gingerly (pun fully intended) to the age of 15. One day, I got a call at lunchtime from my mom, she and my dad were ready to say goodbye. As the three kids had moved out of the house, the primary ownership and care fell on my parents, and we had agreed that their call was the right call even though it was hard. We made an appointment to see the vet on a

Saturday. We thought a traditional McDonald's dinner would be her pick and a perfect last meal before doggy heaven. We loved that dog.

As we said our goodbyes, I looked around the room. I saw my sister who was married, my brother who was approaching 30, my boyfriend who joined us to wish her off because she was important to him, and we were important to him. Great boyfriend, huh? And I saw my parents. I hadn't noticed until then that they had aged too. We had all aged.

We left the veterinarian devastated. We decided to honor her life, celebrate her life, and remember her fondly. Because we were now all adults, we decided to go for a drink. It was Gin and Sodas all around.

As time went on, there were still strong memories of Ginger, but a lot of it is also blurry. But I can still feel her. I cherish the time we had together, the lessons learned, the tender moments, and the connection of family. There are also so many moments that pass and that we never revisit. Yet, these are the moments that make up who we are and most likely, what we stand for in life.

LESSON 3

Time is fleeting, so be present. Dive into the moments that matter, hug your loved ones tight. Focus on the work that makes you happy; find your passion. Live with zeal and be *all in* because time passes so quickly. Be present in your day-to-day and hold onto and cherish great memories, because you never know when you will want to relive those moments. And they are the moments that built you.

HOW DOGS MAKE US BETTER HUMANS

My mom was selfless when she decided to let us have a dog. It was this one dog that inspired my mom to let go of old fears. Because of this very act, we all got to experience and love our girl, Ginger. Our family love got stronger the day Ginger came into our lives. You can't get any better than that!

PUPPIES AND CHICKENS

Story 15 - Accept What Is

"Dog will be dogs. You can't change their design and why would you want to? Meet them where they stand and love them how they are, and they will show you your greatest gifts and your biggest faults."

— BEA BOHM-MEYER

WRITTEN BY TERRY MEYER STONE

TERRY IS MY BEAUTIFUL AND KIND-HEARTED SISTER-IN-LAW. SHE IS A MOM AND GRANDMA. SHE LIVES ON THE BEAUTIFUL ANARCHIST VINEYARD IN BRITISH COLUMBIA WITH HER HUSBAND ANDREW. SHE IS CURRENTLY PRESIDENT OF

MAYHEM WINES. I ALSO WANT TO SNEAK IN THAT SHE IS A PREVIOUS MISS CANADA!

*A*s I write this, one of my Great Pyrenees/Border Collie Cross 'puppies' is out dragging an irrigation pipe around the yard. On closer inspection, a rabbit is hiding inside that she's trying to flush out. It seems appropriate.

Eleven years ago, in search of the idyllic life that we knew was awaiting us just beyond the horizon - a life of slower pace, closer to the earth, drinking wine, enjoying the heat, and life's richer experiences - we moved to the Okanagan. My brother and wife owned a winery, and we were bitten by the vineyard dream. So, we purchased a small vineyard perched on a hill overlooking Lake Osoyoos in the southernmost part of the Okanagan Valley and the northern tip of the Great Basin Desert. This area is known for sage, rattlesnake, black widows, and heat. With a spectacular view and dreams of long hot nights drinking wine with good friends, we jumped into the vineyard life.

Two city kids with no idea that being on a vineyard was intense, back-breaking, soul-sucking, and stress-inducing farming! Along with us, that first year we acquired a beautiful Husky/Collie cross dog named Murphy, who only loved to live outdoors and protect our property from all real and imagined threats. He was the most handsome and royal of dogs, and all who met him fell in love.

Concerned with the coyotes that roamed freely, we – in our wisdom – acquired another vineyard dog, Maggie to keep Murphy company. Maggie was a rescue Doberman/Lab cross who had a rough start in life. She had suffered from severe mange and was missing much of her hair, was immune challenged, and was a fearful and needy dog. She did end up inside and on the couch most of the time. Her main motivator was food, and she would never, ever let you miss a meal. She did however, bond immediately with Murphy and this team took on all challenges, from gophers, marmots, birds, insects, and a few coyotes. One summer Murphy was bitten on the neck by a rattlesnake and was a very sick dog for three days, but somehow fought off the venom and continued roaming the vineyard as a king should. He was that kind of dog. Several times, Maggie blocked me as I stepped out of my car and wouldn't let me pass until I discovered a rattlesnake in my path, and we managed to walk around.

As these two beautiful dogs began to age, we came up with our next bright idea. We had started raising chickens who roamed freely on the vineyard, but we were losing some to predators; owls, hawks, coyotes, and more, that live on this mountainside, with bears in the fall and the occasional cougar dropping by unannounced. Having heard of the majestic livestock guardian dogs, we decided to get not one, but two Great Pyrenees/Border Collie Cross sisters. We felt if we got them when they were young, they would be mentored by our vineyard dogs, and then when Murphy and Maggie were in their golden years, they could hand over the mantle of guardian and enjoy just snoozing by the fire. Seemed like a brilliant plan.

We found out later that getting two siblings isn't too bright. We also found out later that having two puppies while you have your 3-year-old granddaughter come live with you for nine months isn't too bright either. We seemed surrounded by toddlers of the human and canine kind, along with their accidents, mistakes, energy, and chaos. We named the dogs Calamity Jane and Annie Oakley…also one of our first mistakes, as they were determined to live up to their names. Murphy never accepted them and despite their fawning adulation, would have nothing to do with them. So much for noble mentorship.

"Callie and Oakley" were mostly confined to the deck in front of our house to protect them from predators while Murphy and Maggie remained the leaders of the pack. The chickens still wandered freely. When we decided that the puppies were now old enough, they'd be safe to roam the vineyard unsupervised (daytime only), we set them free. That week they killed a chicken and dragged it back up to the deck. What? Our great protectors turned into our biggest threat! This plan was not working out.

We immediately locked up the chickens in their run and took the dogs with us daily to feed them and care for them. We let them know that these chickens were part of the family and required their protection. After six months, we released the chickens on a beautiful summer day, and my guardian protectors killed them all within the first six hours. We were stunned and dismayed. How could these guardians be so blood-thirsty and wrong? We started to think that we were not raising domestic companions, but feral predators. You must understand though, they are gentle giants. So sweet, so compliant, so good with children, so smart and, we thought, easy to train. They were like undercover assassins and the chickens were their assignment. We did not replace the chickens.

For the next two years, we tried to keep those puppies on the property but putting two Pyrenees on a mountain backing onto a reserve area was impossible. We would consistently go around and fill in the fence holes where they dug out and coyotes and bears dug in (the bears love eating grapes), but to no avail. Finally, we put a GPS on the dogs, and followed their adventures up the mountain, travelling over 15 km a day.

Last year, we had to say goodbye to our two beautiful older dogs, Maggie early in the year and Murphy just after Christmas. They had been loyal, noble companions and it broke our hearts to part with them. It seems that since that time, or maybe it's just that they are now nearing 4 years old, my two 'puppies' have become more settled. They now only rarely wander off property, and usually just if they are chasing a deer or coyote. I've watched them happily chase a coyote all through our vineyard. The wily coyote won the race. Occasionally they'll disappear and then start dragging in deer parts. I'm pretty sure they've just found another critter's kill and are not out there bringing down larger beasts than our chickens. At least that's what I really hope.

I still miss our chickens. I loved watching them with their colorful plumage wander freely through the vines. I loved getting fresh eggs daily. In some ways, they represented the dream; our new lifestyle that was hard fought for. But like with all fantasies, there comes a day of reconciliation with reality. Our new reality is two white fluffy dogs with their deceptively calm and peaceful personalities. They are not bouncy like a Labs; they are not fiercely active like Huskies. If not running, they don't sit. They simply drop wherever they are. They love to lay in the snow and the colder it is outside, the happier they are. They like their food, but they are indifferent to when you feed them.

In many ways, they have taught me to accept that which is, that which is unchangeable and immutable. The nature of a predator, be it rattlesnake, hawk or coyote, or fluffy white puppy, has its role in our farm life. I love these two dogs and somehow, they know that they have big shoes to fill and are doing their best to grow into them. With our other two dogs gone, they have taken up the positions of protector and companion, just as we planned. They have taught me to love unconditionally, even that which I don't understand nor want, but to accept their fierce and loving nature. I like to think that we have provided them the best possible life to fulfill their purpose as guardians of the mountain, to roam freely and protect our property, and to, above all, be free.

HOW DOGS MAKE US BETTER HUMANS

Not everything is controllable. "In many ways, they have taught me to accept that which is, that which is unchangeable and immutable." I never meant to put the chickens at risk. It is a good reminder that dogs are dogs. They are not human and can't rationalize instinct. We humans must know and accept that.

CITY DOG VERSUS COUNTRY DOG

Story 16 - Be Unique

"Every dog is unique because every dog has something to teach you."

— BEA BOHM-MEYER

WRITTEN BY VICKY ANDRESS

VICKY IS ONE OF MY DEAREST FRIENDS. SHE HAS HAD A LONG AND DISTINGUISHED CAREER SUPPORTING AND EMPOWERING INDIVIDUALS WITH DISABILITIES AND HAS RECENTLY RETIRED. WE WALK OUR DOGS TOGETHER ALMOST EVERY DAY. SHE IS ONE OF THE KINDEST AND MOST GENEROUS PEOPLE I KNOW.

$\mathcal{I}$t all started over 15 years ago. Well, more than that. My name is Vicky, and I married my husband Cam over 35 years ago. We have 3 beautiful daughters named Genevieve, Kate, and Georgia is our youngest. I should also note that I am Bea's best friend. Our families are bonded for life because of our girls and because of our dogs. This is our story.

Our 3 daughters started asking for a dog almost as soon as they could talk. When Georgia was in elementary school her teacher shared with us that her storytelling and writing were excellent, but we really had to sway her to write about something other than a dog. Prior to Christmas one year, I approached Cam with what I said would be the final time that I would ask about getting a dog. He relented, saying that he would not be responsible for walking, feeding, or cleaning up after "it."

Our Labradoodle joined our family just in time for Christmas; the best gift we have ever given or received. We set up the video camera to capture the moment. Genevieve and Kate were so thrilled and excited, but Georgia's reaction surprised us. She didn't say a word. She just stood there and stared. Later she explained that all that she could think was, I GOT A DOG, I GOT A DOG. I FINALLY GOT A DOG.

The girls named the dog Marley (it was before Marley and Me). Marley was a girl, and she was adorable. We told our friends and parents that we named her after Jacob Marley because it was Christmas. The truth is we named her after Bob Marley because she came with a hemp collar. I also knew Cam was thinking, "Oh great, another female in the house."

Marley was my first dog, and it is difficult to find words to describe her or to share how she enriched our family. Our friends would say "Marley is People." Marley was pure love.

Bea's family and ours spent a lot of time together. It is ironic that our family was the first to get a dog, yet today their family is all about dogs. During the early days, our children conspired and convinced Dan and Bea that they needed a dog in their lives too. I will be honest, for that to occur, we had to promise to babysit the dog if they ever went out of town. Charlie was the first Bohm-Meyer family dog. Now, not only were Bea and I best friends, and our daughters were best friends, but our dogs became best friends. They say your life is more meaningful when you have deep connections. Well, we were well connected.

Marley not only had the handle "people dog" but also was called the "city dog." She would walk on the sidewalk or trail while Charlie ran in and out of the bushes like a country dog. Marley would do her business and immediately return indoors. She didn't like to be far from Cam or me. As a matter of fact, we had no fences in the back yard and she never once left the yard, other than to visit with our next-door neighbor when she was on her deck. Marley was very praise-focused and loved to be around people.

We were devastated when we unexpectedly lost Marley. This hit us all extremely hard. I didn't expect it and the loss left a hole in our hearts that we feel even to this day. It hit Cam the hardest. Mister "I am not going to be responsible for walking, feeding, or cleaning up after it." Yet it was him who walked her every day, fed her, and cleaned up after her. It was him who put a bench at the front window in his office so they could spend their days together and that Marley could look out the window and wait for us to come home. And it was him who taught Marley everything about the Edmonton Oilers hockey team. Marley even had a blue mohawk when the Oilers were in the playoffs. As the girls got older and went on with their own lives at a distance, we were glad that Marley was still a part of our home.

The loss was so devastating that Cam didn't want another dog. I convinced him while we were on a holiday that we did need a dog in our lives, but that we should wait. We returned from holidays to an empty house. I remember it well. The feeling of emptiness, no sound of excitement when we walked in the door. Where was the love that used to greet us? It was the only thing that made you want to return home from a holiday.

The next day on my way to work, Cam showed me a picture of a Labradoodle with a big red bow tie. Lola (named after Great Grandma Lola) came into our lives the next day. So much for waiting.

It was very difficult for us to get used to a puppy again, and to have a dog that was not Marley. Lola was the exact opposite in personality and temperament to Marley. Lola was a little bit *country* and Marley was a lot *city*. Marley was calm, gentle, and loved to be petted. Marley was almost human. Lola was energetic and crazy. I had forgotten the puppy phase. Nonetheless, Lola had big paws to fill.

Lola was the same breed as Marley, the same colouring, and the same size, but she has a tail that curls up like a pig's tail. Bonding took a while, but Lola did not give up on us. It took time, but we started to appreciate her for who she was; a happy, fun-loving, very quirky, and very kind dog. She was not Marley. She was Lola.

Cam works from home these days and I am retired now. She is my companion and the motivation to go for long walks every day. Her excitement for our daily routine makes me excited to get out and about. She is my fitness trainer and my friend.

We now have two grandchildren, and they love Lola to the moon. She returns that love with hugs, kisses, play, and protection. When our grandson was just beginning to crawl, he started to make his way down our stairs. Lola circled him on each stair. I wonder if she was just as nervous as I was, watching him go. I loved she was there for him, protecting him.

Lola loves to travel with us. Whenever possible, we take her on our trips. She has been to more places than some people, including Florida, Ontario, Jasper, and Canmore. She is a water dog. She's swam in the Gulf of Mexico, St Lawrence River, Lake Edith, and the North Saskatchewan River. She even loves boating. When we cannot take her with us, one of our kids willingly volunteers to stay with her. When that is not possible, she loves to stay with The Leash Team. She adores her stays with Dan and Bea so much that we started referring to it as "Doggy Disneyland."

Our two dogs brought joy and love into our home. They were so different in so many ways. City dog versus bush and water dog. Marley was motivated by praise and Lola, by food. Marley loved to snuggle and be petted. Lola, for the longest time, would duck away when you tried to pet her. Marley would daintily lick the outside of her water bowl; Lola puts her entire face in it and leaves a trail of water throughout the house. What they have in common is unconditional love, both giving and receiving.

So here we are now, many years later. Thanks to Marley, Dan and Bea got their first dog, Charlie. Then they got another dog, and then a third. They eventually opened an off-leash dog walking and training business called The Leash Team. Today they have over 300 walks a week, they have a thriving family business that they are passionate about, and Bea is writing a book about dogs. You're welcome. We do not want to take all the credit; however, we do think Marley would expect a dedication note in your book.

HOW DOGS MAKE US BETTER HUMANS

We have learned that no dog or human can replace another, and that is okay. Loss is part of life, but you can't shut the door. If we had shut the door, we would not have Lola. Lola is not Marley and that is the gift. Each is unique and special. Marley and Lola reminded us that our authentic selves are a gift to the world and each other. We should never compare who we are to others. Instead, we should each honor our authenticity.

BEA'S TOP 9 THINGS LEARNED FROM BEING A DOG MOM

BEA'S TOP 9 THINGS LEARNED FROM BEING A DOG MOM

I am not a dog trainer. I do not claim to have formal dog training knowledge. The 9 points below are things I have picked up on as a dog mom. They are important to me and may help you if you have a dog or want to adopt a dog. I have learned these concepts on my own and from people who are knowledgeable and passionate about dogs and work with dogs for a living. I share these with you, not as a professional, but from my own experience.

My personal experience with dogs has also taught me to work with a credible dog trainer. If you want to be knowledgeable about your dog and want a well-behaved, happy fur ball that is connected to you and your family and friends, a trainer is a must.

I encourage you to explore these 9 points with a dog trainer or a professional in the canine industry.

1. DO RESEARCH ON YOUR DOG'S BREED

Dogs have been associated with humans for over 15,000 years. They have been companions, protectors, and workers. Knowing the breed of your dog can help you understand the size, temperament, behavior, and even triggers. I had to learn that Eddie, a Pyrenees/Maremma mix gets grumpy when a dog comes to our house. This makes sense since the Maremma part in her is the inherited protector. Eddie only stays grumpy for 5 minutes, but her behavior is communicating "This is my house, play nice and you are welcome to be part of the family." It took our trainer to help interpret this behavior. This is very much aligned with her breed, which is a herder and protector. Different breeds of dogs exist because they were bred to address a particular role in serving humans. The best dog experience and relationship happens when you know how your dog will fit into your lifestyle. Knowing how your dog shows up in the world creates a deeper understanding of mutual needs and a great connection in your relationship.

Understanding your dog means understanding the breed. I really do think this is one of the most important things you should know as a dog owner.

2. HIRE A GREAT – NOT A GOOD, BUT A GREAT DOG TRAINER

There is nothing more rewarding than a well-behaved dog. We have an off-leash dog walking company. We also train dogs, but not while on the walks. My husband trains dogs and yet we hired one of our own dog trainers to help train our dogs. Why? Because we are too close to our dogs. Trainers will see things we do not. They hold us accountable for doing the work. Dog training is serious business. A great dog trainer does not only train your dog, they train you.

We believe in force-free and fear-free training. I personally feel this methodology elevates your relationship with your dog and really helps grow confidence. It is also important to know training never stops. It is a journey. It is just like having a child; you never stop teaching your kids. Do not assume you can go to a few puppy classes, and it is done. It is never done. Bringing a dog into your family is a lifelong journey and relationship.

3. CALMING ENERGY CAN HELP DE-ESCALATE EXUBERANCE

Do you ever walk into your house and your dog gets very excited to see you? During those moments it seems they may go a little nuts. Well, that may be your fault. No worries. I fall into that trap. Who does not get excited to see me, ha-ha?! In general, it is my energy that escalates the exuberance. We have the privilege of having many dogs visit our house. For the most part, when dogs visit our home, they are excited. Too much exuberance can turn to aggression if you are not careful. Every dog is different; some dogs love energetic and in-your-face greetings, while others do not. The first rule I learned from my husband: the human must be calm. Dogs take their cues from you. The same goes for stress. If you take your dog for a walk and you are stressed, your dog will feed off your energy and feel the stress. This may result in less-than-ideal dog behavior. Make no mistake, dogs feel deeply and read energy better than they understand verbal commands. Dan can walk 12 dogs off-leash with non-verbal commands. It seems the dogs can read his mind. Really, the dogs are reading his energy and body language. It is extraordinary to watch.

If dogs are too exuberant on the group walks, he gently separates them with a signal or verbal cue. At times he may put them on a leash and help them walk side by side with him until they are calm. He rewards calm behavior with treats and love. I have observed this over and over again and practice it when I need to with my pups. Separate-Distract-Reward.

4. PERSONAL ENERGY IS EVERYTHING

This is something I learned early on. Humans use words to communicate. Dogs respond to energy. Energy and smell are how dogs, and most animals, communicate. Dogs read and feel your intention and respond accordingly. It may seem they understand your words but, for the most part, they are responding to your intention. The general rule for me is you reward a dog with great praise and happiness and the dog feels happy. If you are frustrated with a dog, the dog will feel frustrated. Most importantly, if you are nervous, your dog will be nervous and that might lead to some nervous behavior. Energy is everything. If one of my dogs is misbehaving, I try to stay calm. I distract them rather than say no or get mad. They hear "No" all too often in many conversations directed at them or around them. It can be confusing. When I can distract and have my dogs follow my command, I reward them with a treat or big-time love. Love means good. Loves means I am not giving off bad energy. Dan used to tease me that I could not be an official dog walker because I worry too much. That worry would impact the dog's good energy. It is a fair point.

5. UNDERSTAND YOUR DOG'S BEHAVIOR

Dogs are always talking to you. Whether they are telling you they love you, if they are stressed, or if they are frustrated. How a dog feels is expressed in their behavior. For example, as a dog parent, it is 100% your responsibility to watch for dog behaviors that may escalate into something undesirable. Dog fights seldom happen out of the blue. Dogs show you they are escalating. They have no ability to reason. That means it can only show up as fight or flight. Things to watch out for in all circumstances, but especially at off-leash parks.

- High energy dogs coming or going
- People coming or going
- High activity games such as group fetch or chase

For example, I know my dog Eddie is a protector and herder. She is triggered by high-energy dogs running by her, especially as she gets out of the car. I have learned from our trainer to keep Eddie on the leash until she feels calm and safe and knows this is a place for a fun walk. I manage the threat and the fight or flight is off the table.

6. UNDERSTAND THE SIGNS OF DOG STRESS

Stress shows up in many ways. This is something I did not know as a new dog mom. It is our responsibility to be alert to circumstances and the environment. Stress signals may show up and we may read them as normal.

Panting, shedding, not taking treats, licking, barking, and salivating may show up for you as normal. In some circumstances, it might be normal. In certain circumstances, these behaviors and others are signs that something is not quite right. Obvious warning signs that are easily detected are vomiting, tense muscles, barking and raised hackles (the fur on the back of the neck that runs down the backbone). Just a reminder, your dog is always talking to you. Read your environment and listen to your dog. I did not realize that Buckley pants when he is stressed, and he also pants when he is hot. I need to know the difference so I can manage the situation.

7. YOUR DOG CAN SMELL BETTER THAN YOU CAN

We humans have about 6 million olfactory receptors in our noses. Dogs have more than 300 million. They breathe in through their nostrils and exhale through the slits on the sides of their noses. That means they are constantly processing what is happening around them. They can smell when something is not quite right. They are sensitive to changes in energy and intuitive to different emotions. Scent and the act of smelling also helps them process this information. These attributes are highly regarded and valued in working dogs.

I walked with a fire chief in the off-leash park one day. His amazing dog had a badge on his collar. I asked why. The dog was a fire captain. His job was to sniff out the causes of fires. He explained to me his dog can smell one part per trillion (ppt) (1), which is three times more sensitive than today's technology and detection instruments, and he believes a dog's ability to smell is more reliable.

I have also witnessed dogs getting out of their owner's car and running half a kilometer to Dan. There was no line of sight and they had to run through a park and in between trees to get to him. Did they feel his energy, or did they smell him? I don't know. All I know is that those dogs knew Dan was in the park. I have also been told that dogs can smell something that has already happened. They can smell if you have been there and gone. If you experience your dog picking up a scent, let them sniff. It is part of how they decipher the information. Sniffing and smelling are part of their process that not only feeds them information, but it also provides brain stimulation. Yes, there is a time for them to walk with you and a time for them to sniff and explore. They need both.

8. A GPS IS GREAT FOR OFF-LEASH WALKS

We often walk our dogs in the river valley in areas where they can be off leash. Our dogs are well-behaved and know the rules of walking with us. They have great recall, do not wander off, and are typically polite to other walkers, whether human or canine. That does not mean things can't happen. The sight of a rabbit or coyote can trigger a chase. Getting distracted by another dog who wants to play or seeing someone they know may take them off the path and away from you. Some dogs get spooked by thunder or fireworks and will not only run but hide. We put a GPS on our dogs at all times if they are off leash. It gives us peace of mind that we can track them at any time if need be. Dan also uses GPS trackers on all the dogs when walking with The Leash Team. It is a safety tool that also provides peace of mind.

9. EVERYTHING IS ABOUT UNCONDITIONAL LOVE

Dogs respond to you. Love them unconditionally all the time. Love them like crazy when they are good. Distract them when they do something wrong. Be grateful when they teach us patience. I believe when they do something that frustrates us, it is because they are teaching us patience. It is my book, so is it my opinion, and I say love your dogs unconditionally all the time. Your reward will be more than you can ever imagine.

FINAL THOUGHTS

Well, here we are at the end of the book. I hope these stories have touched your heart, tickled your funny bone, and reminded you how precious life is when we are in the presence of our furry friends from the canine world.

It has been a wonderful experience to connect with so many dog lovers, through family, friends, The Leash Team, and those who participated in the survey. Since this project began, many of you continue to bring forward incredible and heartfelt dog stories. These stories are all precious. Who knows, there may be another book!

In the next chapter, you will find a personal 12-page journal. I encourage you to document one lesson you learn from your dog each month; a lesson that makes you a better human; one that you don't want to forget. It will be a great way to cherish the memories.

In the meantime, please keep sharing with me and those around you. These shared journeys are a form of love that connects us to what is good in the world.

It was an added bonus for me personally, to write a book combining my two greatest passions in life, dogs and leadership (in this case self-leadership). I will be honest, there were some who said it couldn't be done. I was told combining the two topics would not make any sense. Yet, I did it.

These stories come from the heart. They are authentic and real and meaningful. I hope they are an everyday reminder to be more conscious, honor the present moment, and enjoy the little moments, because these moments are bigger than you think. Most importantly, I will let you draw your own conclusions from what we can all learn from a dog's purpose and their unconditional love; you may even discover something about yourself through the process.

For me, it all started with a friend who said, "Yes you can." It continued with the unconditional love of a few friends who believed in my idea and believed in me.

So, one final thought before you go on to the 12-page journal and peek at some of the documented research in the appendix:

"Yes, you can."

*To share stories about your dogs, please message The Leash Team on theleashteam.com/contact-us or @theleashteam on Instagram.

HOW DOGS MAKE US BETTER HUMANS: A CHALLENGE

How has your dog(s) made you a better human?

Each month for a year, I challenge you to write down - in the pages that follow - something you have learned from your dog that has taught you about being a better human. These notes will become irreplaceable memories for you to have forever, and can be lovingly shared with family, friends, children and grandchildren.

If it so moves you, share your lessons with The Leash Team at theleashteam.com/contact-us or through Instagram @theleashteam.

LESSON 1

What I learned from my dog(s) this month

Date: _____

LESSON 2

What I learned from my dog(s) this month

Date: _____

LESSON 3

What I learned from my dog(s) this month

Date: _____

LESSON 4

What I learned from my dog(s) this month

Date: _____

LESSON 5

What I learned from my dog(s) this month

Date: _____

LESSON 6

What I learned from my dog(s) this month

Date: _____

LESSON 7

What I learned from my dog(s) this month

Date: _____

LESSON 8

What I learned from my dog(s) this month

Date: _____

LESSON 9

What I learned from my dog(s) this month

Date: _____

LESSON 10

What I learned from my dog(s) this month

Date: _____

LESSON 11

What I learned from my dog(s) this month

Date: _____

LESSON 12

What I learned from my dog(s) this month

Date: _____

APPENDIX
Research Data

The following are some of the research results we received from the survey we sent out. I bet some of this will give you an emotional response! It did for us.

QUESTION: WHY DO YOU OWN A DOG?

I LOVE PETS, I BELIEVE IN RESCUES, AND THEY ARE FAMILY MEMBERS.

A WAGGING TAIL AND KISSES WHEN WE COME HOME. COMPANIONSHIP. A REASON TO GET OUT AND WALK EVERY DAY.

A BEING TO CARE FOR (NOT JUST MY HUSBAND!); OUR HOUSE WAS SO EMPTY WITHOUT ONE.

BECAUSE I GREW UP WITH THEM AND REALIZED HOW MUCH

HAPPINESS THEY BRING TO MY OWN LIFE AND HOW, BY ADOPTING, I CAN IMPROVE THE LIFE OF AT LEAST A FEW DOGS.

DOGS HAVE ENRICHED MY LIFE BOTH PHYSICALLY AND MENTALLY. I WILL NEVER NOT HAVE A DOG.

MY WIFE AND I MET LATE IN LIFE AND DECIDED NOT TO START OUR OWN FAMILY AND HAVING A PUPPY / DOG WAS THE NEXT BEST THING. THE REASONS ARE ENDLESS, FROM THE UNCONDITIONAL LOVE, TO HELPING RELIEVE STRESS, TO MAKING YOU BE MORE ACTIVE. IT'S ALSO NICE TO HAVE COMPANY IN THE HOUSE WHEN THE OTHER IS AWAY.

MY SON HAS ALWAYS WANTED A DOG AND I BUCKLED.... LOL

COMPANY, LOVE OF DOGS, LOVE OF SPECIAL NEEDS DOGS, JUST BECAUSE.

FOR MY KIDS, THE DOG IS A COMPANION FOR OUR FAMILY.

I LOVE THEIR SPIRIT.

AT THE TIME WE GOT OURS, WE WERE IN AN EMOTIONALLY TOUGH PERIOD AND WERE LOOKING TO BRING JOY INTO OUR FAMILY LIFE.

QUESTION: WHAT ARE THE TOP 1 – 3 THINGS YOU HAVE LEARNED FROM YOUR DOG(S)?

LOYALTY, LIVE IN THE NOW, VALUE OF COMPANIONSHIP.

HAVE A POOP BAG IN EVERY POCKET. MY LUNCH IS NEVER JUST MY LUNCH. DOGS ARE VERY SMART. OLLIE SOMEHOW KNOWS WHEN OUR FRIEND IS TEXTING TO GO FOR A WALK. A PET AND A SCRATCH MAKE US BOTH FEEL GOOD.

HOW INTUITIVE THEY ARE. FAITHFUL AND UNCONDITIONAL.

PATIENCE.

UNCONDITIONAL LOVE, FORGIVENESS, AND PATIENCE. THE JOY OF BEING IS ALSO SOMETHING I AM STILL LEARNING FROM THEM.

UNCONDITIONALLY LOVE, THEY FORGIVE YOU NO MATTER WHAT, THEY GET OVER THINGS QUICKLY AND MOVE ON.

UNCONDITIONAL LOVE. THE GREETING OF DOGGIE KISSES AND A TAIL WAGGING NON-STOP EACH TIME YOU ARRIVE HOME, CAN NEVER GET OLD. THEIR ABILITY TO COMFORT. WITH A FAMILY MEMBER WITH ADVANCED DEMENTIA, IT IS A JOY TO WATCH THEM INTERACT, WITH THEIR CLOSENESS TO THAT PERSON. THEY SEEM TO SENSE THAT THINGS AT HOME AREN'T QUITE THE SAME, WITH OUTSIDE CARE COMING AND GOING. MY

HUSBAND WRAPS HER IN A BLANKET AT BEDTIME, AS IF SHE'S A BABY.

EVEN WHEN I GET MAD AT HIM, HE STILL REMAINS HAPPY.

TO ENJOY THE MOMENT. SIMPLE PLEASURES. LOVE UNCONDITIONALLY.

WHAT UNCONDITIONAL LOVE LOOKS LIKE. PATIENCE (YOU HAVE TO GO PEE AGAIN??).

EVERY DAY THERE IS SOMETHING TO WAG YOUR TAIL ABOUT. LOVE IS ON EVERY STEP; WE JUST HAVE TO OPEN OUR HEARTS TO IT. KINDNESS AND ACCEPTANCE ARE THE WAY TO HAPPINESS.

GIVE LOTS OF LOVE. NAPS IN THE SUNSHINE ARE WONDERFUL. WALKS IN NATURE ARE WONDERFUL.

DON'T LEAVE FOOD NEAR THE EDGE OF THE COUNTER. DON'T LEAVE THE RUBBISH BIN OPEN OR UNCOVERED. IF THERE IS SOMETHING ROTTEN/DEAD WITHIN 5 MILES, THEY WILL FIND IT. EAT IT AND ROLL IN IT.

THEY LOVE UNCONDITIONALLY. THEY MAKE YOU SMILE.

TO ENJOY THE OUTDOORS.

DEVOTION, FORGIVENESS, AND THE IMPORTANCE OF AFFECTION AND PRAISE.

Unconditional love and patience.

Our dog is a rescue, so I've learned to be patient and the benefits of routine.

QUESTION: WHAT HAS BEEN YOUR GREATEST CHALLENGE AS A DOG OWNER?

When they die.

It was saying goodbye.

Shedding.

We have a new baby in the house, and I don't want the dog to feel left out — she needs cuddles and love too.

She's a barker, and I have tried hard to teach her to be less vocal.

Being tied down.

Learning to go past my human egocentricity and to create a balance when my dogs' needs have been in conflict with my own.

Managing discipline with my tendency to spoil and overindulge.

THE TOUGHEST PART IS LEAVING HIM BEHIND WHEN WE GO AWAY ON VACATION. WE LOVE TO TRAVEL BUT HAVE CRAMPED OUR STYLE OFTEN, AS WE DON'T WANT TO LEAVE HIM BEHIND. WHEN WE DO GO AWAY WITHOUT HIM, I SPEND EVERY DAY WORRYING ABOUT HIM.

CLEANING UP AFTER HIM AND GETTING OUT OF THE PUPPY STAGE. IT'S LIKE HAVING A TODDLER AGAIN.

DOG HAIR (HAHA). LOSING A BEST FRIEND AND SOUL MATE.

QUESTION: WHAT HAS BEEN YOUR GREATEST REWARD AS A DOG OWNER?

WHEN THEY SEE YOU AFTER YOU'VE BEEN GOING FOR A WHILE.

BEING GREETED AT THE DOOR WITH A WAGGING TAIL. HAVING A HAPPY, LOVING DOG.

SENSE OF SECURITY, NEVER FEELING ALONE.

SEEING OUR DOG BECOME MORE RELAXED AROUND US AND MORE CONFIDENT AROUND STRANGERS.

THE LOVE YOU FEEL FOR THEM, HOW THEY TRULY ARE A MEMBER OF THE FAMILY, THE CALMING EFFECT SHE HAS WHEN YOU ARE STRESSED.

HAVING UNCONDITIONAL LOVE.

THEIR AFFECTION, BEING WITNESS AND GUARDIAN TO THEIR
MOMENTS OF PLAY, FREEDOM IN NATURE AND HAPPINESS, THE
POSSIBILITY TO LEARN TO COMMUNICATE NONVERBALLY WITH
AND UNDERSTAND A CREATURE OF A DIFFERENT SPECIES.

WATCHING OUR KIDS LOVE OUR DOG AND GROW WITH
THE DOG.

OPENING OF THE HEART.

ENCOURAGES US TO GET OUT EVEN IN EDMONTON WEATHER.
IT IS A HAPPY TIME WHEN YOU ARE OUT WITH THE DOGS AND
WATCH THEM PLAY.

HAVING SUCH AN AFFECTIONATE GOOFBALL TO COME HOME TO
EVERY DAY. HE'S ALWAYS SUPER HAPPY TO SEE MOM. HE
BRIGHTENS MY MOOD, NO MATTER WHAT KIND OF DAY
I'VE HAD!

THE UNCONDITIONAL LOVE THAT A DOG BRINGS TO THE
FAMILY.

THE LOVE AND LAUGHS.

THE JOY HE BRINGS TO US WHEN HE GREETS US AT THE DOOR.
THE COMPANIONSHIP HE OFFERS.

QUESTION: WHAT DO YOU THINK YOU GIVE BACK TO YOUR DOG(S)?

CARE, SAFETY, LOVE. A GOOD LIFE.

THE FEELING OF SECURITY AND BELONGING, HE IS PART OF OUR PACK.

COMPANIONSHIP, LOVE, AND FUN

LOVING HOME.

LOVE IN RETURN. BY KEEPING THEM WELL AND FED AND BATHED, ETC., AND INCLUDING THEM IN YOUR ACTIVITIES. SHE IS CRAZY ABOUT CAR RIDES, SO SHE IS TAKEN MOST OF THE TIME. SHE LOVES TO GO TO OUR FAMILIES' HOMES.

FOOD, SHELTER, AND ATTENTION.

MY CARE, MY ATTENTION, AND MY LOVE, BUT SOMETIMES IT FEELS LIKE I FALL SHORT.

WE RESCUED HER! WE LOVE HER, SHE HAS A GREAT HOME, SHE GETS A MILLION WALKS.

UNCONDITIONAL LOVE AND AFFECTION.

SAFETY, LOVE AND AFFECTION, NOURISHMENT, SENSE OF BELONGING AND SECURITY.

Hopefully the same as what she gives to us.

I give him all the love I can by taking excellent care of him. We have taken him to multiple vets for his condition to get the best possible care. We walk him and exercise him regularly. I prepare special meals in my slow cooker. He enjoys rare dog food, such as sweet potato, kangaroo, and rabbit. He sleeps in bed at night.

Love, food, shelter, balls, The Leash Team.

Our full attention & response to her wants (treats) & needs (careful handling of her achy joints).

Love, appreciation, acceptance, support, partnership, belonging, and happy times together.

I hope they know how much I love them. I take them on adventures and holidays to the ocean.

QUESTION: DO YOU THINK YOUR DOG(S) HAS A PURPOSE?

A part of the family; they teach young people respon-sibility.

Well, if you ask Oliver, it's to let everyone who walks past our house know he lives here, and to kiss everyone who comes to visit. He is our living security system,

*AND OUR BEST BUD. LIFE WOULD NOT BE THE SAME WITHOUT
HIM. TO FIND AND EAT FOOD. TO LIVE A LIFE WHERE LOVE
AND HAPPINESS PREVAILS.*

*SOME DAYS, I THINK WE'RE ALL JUST CREATURES GOING
ABOUT LIFE THE BEST WE CAN. OTHER TIMES, I FEEL
CONNECTED TO A HIGHER PURPOSE OF LEARNING TO SHARE
THIS EARTH AND LIFETIME TOGETHER, AND THAT'S WHERE
DOGS COME IN AS FAITHFUL COMPANIONS AND GUIDES. THEY
BRING US BACK TO THE IMPORTANCE OF BEING PART OF
NATURE AND REKINDLE AN APPRECIATION OF SIMPLICITY, IN
THE MIDST OF SOCIETIES THAT ARE HECTIC AND TAKE US AWAY
FROM THAT. COMPANIONSHIP, LOVE FOR THEIR FAMILY
LOYALTY, PLEASING YOU — WE HAVE A FRIEND WHO IS DYING
AND HIS DOG (LARGE DOG) LAYS IN BED WITH HIM AND PUTS
HIS HEAD ON HIS PILLOW AND HE HAS SAID IT COMFORTS HIM.*

*TO ENJOY A HAPPY, LOVING HOME WHERE SHE CAN LOVE, PLAY
AND, IN OUR CASE, BE ON "GUARD."*

*TO LET PEOPLE KNOW THAT SPECIAL NEEDS IS ONLY IN THE
EYE OF THE BEHOLDER.*

COMPANIONSHIP & SIMPLE HAPPINESS.

FAMILY. COMPANION. PROTECT. PLAY.

UNCONDITIONAL LOVE.

TO BRING JOY TO EVERYONE.

BE HAPPY.

TEACHING US TO LIVE IN THE MOMENT.

GIVING US LOVE & LAUGHTER WHEN WE NEED IT MOST.

SHE REMINDS ME TO LIVE IN THE PRESENT.

TO KEEP OUR FAMILY CLOSE.

QUESTION: HOW DOES YOUR DOG(S) IMPACT YOU, YOUR FAMILY, AND FRIENDS?

THEY GIVE US LOVE, RESPONSIBILITY, JOY, LAUGHTER, CUDDLES.

OLLIE IS ONE OF THE MOST LOVING KID-FRIENDLY DOGS I HAVE EVER OWNED. OUR FAMILY AND FRIENDS HAVE FALLEN IN LOVE WITH HIM. OUR NEIGHBOURS' GRANDKIDS WOULD COME OVER TO PLAY WITH HIM IN THE SUMMER. FIVE KIDS CHASING HIM AROUND THE YARD, HE WAS SO GENTLE WITH THEM. ONE OF OUR GRANDKIDS IS AUTISTIC AND HE AND OLLIE ARE AMAZING TOGETHER, OLLIE LISTENS TO HIM SO WELL.

TOPIC OF CONVERSATION. TEACHES RESPONSIBILITIES TO THE CHILDREN TO CARE FOR AN ANIMAL.

MY PARENTS REALLY ENJOY HAVING HER TO VISIT. IT CAN SOMETIMES BE CHALLENGING TO STRUCTURE OUR OUTINGS TO

ENSURE THE DOG ISN'T IN THE CAR FOR TOO LONG OR AT HOME BY HERSELF FOR TOO LONG.

MY GREATEST SOURCE OF HAPPINESS.

THEY'RE PART OF THE FAMILY. SO, EVERY DECISION REGARDING OUR HOME INCLUDES THEM.

TEACHES RESPONSIBILITY TO MY SON.

MAKES OUR LIVES BETTER EVERY DAY.

OUR DOG MAKES US THINK ABOUT SOMETHING OUTSIDE OF OURSELVES. TO REMEMBER TO BE THERE FOR SOMETHING THAT MATTERS AND TO TAKE TIME TO ENJOY SIMPLE PLEASURES.

SHE MAKES OUR FAMILY WHOLE. ALL MY FRIENDS ARE SO EXCITED TO SEE HER. SHE EVEN GETS SOME OFFICE DAYS.

HE BRINGS JOY AND MAKES US LAUGH.

THE ARE A PART OF MY FAMILY & FRIENDS. THEY DO EVERYTHING WITH US.

THERE IS A CULTURE OF DOG OWNERS IN OUR NEIGHBOUR-HOOD. WE HAVE MET MANY FRIENDLY PEOPLE AND WE ALL HAVE THE SAME 'DOG' THING IN COMMON. THESE ARE PEOPLE WE WOULD NEVER HAVE GOTTEN TO KNOW WITHOUT CHARLY. THE MORE WE ARE OUT AND ABOUT, THE MORE THEY GET TO KNOW CHARLY, AND HE THEM. ONE OF OUR DAUGHTERS HAS A

DOG AND OTHER DOES NOT. THE LATTER HAS 4 CHILDREN AND THEY LITERALLY ADOPTED CHARLY AS THEIR OWN. THEY ARE STRONGLY THINKING ABOUT GETTING A PUP OF THEIR OWN. THERE IS A THING ABOUT BEING AROUND OTHER DOG OWNERS/LOVERS. CHARLY HAS BOARDED WITH THE LEASH TEAM ON SEVERAL OCCASIONS, AND HE HAS A BOND WITH THEIR DOG EDDIE. EACH TIME WE WALK THE GOLF COURSE AND PASS CLOSE TO EDDIE'S HOUSE CHARLY PULLS VERY STRONGLY TOWARD THAT YARD. HE KNOWS WHERE HIS BEST FRIEND LIVES AND HE KNOW WHERE THE LEASH TEAM IS. THERE'S LOTS MORE TO THIS BUT CHARLY HAS HAD SUCH AN IMPACT. WHEN HE IS AWAY FOR A DAY/NIGHT, OUR HOME BECOMES 'DEAFINGLY' SILENT WHEN HE ISN'T HERE.

QUESTION: TELL US A GREAT STORY ABOUT YOUR DOG(S)

IT WAS HER FIRST DAY WITH US, A 5-MONTH-OLD PUPPY. TOM PICKED HER UP FROM THE SELLER AND TOOK HER TO THE VET (I HAD WORK). WHEN I ARRIVED HOME, I THOUGHT I WOULD HEAR SOME NOISE, BUT INSTEAD IT WAS SO SILENT. I CAME INTO OUR OFFICE AND SAW THEM BOTH, VALLY AND TOM, ASLEEP ON THE FLOOR BY THE FIREPLACE. WE HAD NO DOG BED THAT DAY, SO SHE JUST HAD A LITTLE BLANKET. IN THAT MOMENT I SAW SOMETHING I HAVE NEVER SEEN BEFORE AND, FROM THAT DAY ON, TOM BECAME A DIFFERENT PERSON. IT WAS CLEARLY A PRIORITY EXERCISE WHEN LOVE, CLOSENESS AND SENSE OF BELONGING MAKES YOU FEEL HAPPY EVEN SLEEPING ON THE FLOOR IF YOU HAVE THE RIGHT PUPPY BY YOUR SIDE :). VALLY DID NOT HAVE TO SLEEP ON THE FLOOR

MUCH SINCE THEN, NOR TOM. BUT THAT SENSE OF LOVE AND
CONNECTION AND DEEPER LEVEL OF EMOTIONAL LIFE NEVER
LEFT OUR HOME. SHE BROUGHT SOMETHING INTANGIBLE FROM
THE FIRST STEPS IN OUR HOUSE, AND YET WE SEE MANIFESTA-
TIONS OF THAT IN OUR RELATIONSHIPS WITH EACH OTHER AND
OURSELVES SO CLEARLY.

I'VE HAD MANY CANINE FRIENDS, FROM THE STRAYS I
BEFRIENDED AS A CHILD IN DIFFERENT COUNTRIES IN ASIA TO
THE DOGS IN SHELTERS I'VE VOLUNTEERED AT, AS WELL AS MY
TWO CURRENT CANINE COMPANIONS, PIMPUZ AND ROTOTOM,
SO IT'S HARD TO CHOOSE ONE GREAT STORY. WHEN I WAS
LIVING IN TAIWAN, I MET A LABRADOR MIX ON THE STREETS
AND SHE FOLLOWED ME HOME. SHE SPENT A WEEK SLEEPING
AT THE DOOR OF THE APARTMENT BUILDING WHERE I LIVED
AND WE WOULD GO ON WALKS TOGETHER EVERY DAY, UNTIL A
COMPLAINT WENT AROUND THE BUILDING ABOUT HER PRES-
ENCE, AND MY FAMILY HELPED ME FIND A HOME FOR HER WITH
SOME FRIENDS. SHE WAS ONE OF THE DOGS THAT TAUGHT ME
HOW SPECIAL A CONNECTION CAN BE BETWEEN A PERSON AND
A DOG, BECAUSE SHE WAS AFRAID OF EVERYONE ELSE AND
WOULDN'T LET ANYONE BUT ME APPROACH HER, WHICH MADE
IT FEEL LIKE AN HONOR TO CHOSEN AS SOMEONE
TRUSTWORTHY.

WHEN OUR DAUGHTER WAS BORN, OUR DOG WAS SO EXCITED.
SHE SLEPT WITH THE BABY'S HAT IN HER BED, AND SHE
WOULDN'T LEAVE THE BABY'S SIDE, EVEN TO GO FOR WALKS.
SHE IS VERY PROTECTIVE OF THE BABY. SHE'LL COME AND

GIVE THE BABY SNIFFS AND LICKS THROUGHOUT THE DAY, TO CHECK THAT SHE'S ALRIGHT.

WHILE LIVING WITH A PERSON WITH SEVERE DEMENTIA, SHE SEEMS TO KNOW THINGS ARE NOT QUITE THE SAME AS BEFORE. GRANDPA CALLS BEDTIME, 'BYLOW' TIME AND MADDY GETS ON THE BED RIGHT AWAY. GRANDPA LOVES TO WRAP HER UP IN HIS UNDERSHIRT, BATH TOWEL, WHATEVER HE THINKS SHE NEEDS TO BE WARM. SOMETIMES IT'S JUST TOO MUCH, AND SHE CRAWLS OUT IN TIME, BUT SHE NEVER SEEMS TO MIND THE REPETITIVE KIND OF LOVE HE SEEMS TO BE GIVING HER.

"RECOLLECT THAT THE ALMIGHTY, WHO GAVE THE DOG TO BE COMPANION OF OUR PLEASURES AND OUR TOILS, HATH INVESTED HER WITH A NATURE NOBLE AND INCAPABLE OF DECEIT." -- SIR WALTER SCOTT, THE TALISMAN, 1825. OUR PREVIOUS DOG ENTERTAINED GUESTS BY SHOWING THEM HOW SHE "TIDIED UP" WHEN IT WAS TIME TO GO TO BED. SHE WAS TRAINED TO PICK UP HER TOYS AND PUT THEM IN HER TOY BASKET. WE HAD MORE LUCK WITH HER THAN THE KIDS. ANOTHER TRICK THAT PEOPLE LOVED TO SEE IS WHEN THEY CAME OVER FOR DINNER, WE WOULD ASK HER TO SAY GRACE. ON DEMAND, SHE WOULD PUT HER FRONT PAWS ON THE CHAIR, BOW HER HEAD. WE WOULD SAY GRACE AND WHEN SHE HEARD THE WORD AMEN, SHE WOULD LIFT UP HER HEAD.

ABOUT THE AUTHOR

Bea Bohm-Meyer has spent two decades walking side by side with business leaders helping them understand how they show up in the world and how to lead their company culture. She feels blessed and honoured to do this work. Along this journey she has learned so much about the fundamental importance of human connection, belonging, and empathy.

Bea's company is known for organizational design and leveraging how to humanize and operationalize culture. Today, in addition to culture design, she is pioneering compassionate leadership in the workplace; helping leaders and employees alike see the world through the lens of others, helping to cultivate deeper connections, and leveraging human uniqueness.

Apart from helping companies build game-changing cultures and growing compassionate leaders, Bea loves mentoring start-up companies and young women who want to make an impact in the world. She sits on various for-profit and not-for-profit Boards loving to be a part of her greater community. At her very core, Bea describes herself as a bleeding heart. As a young girl, she was always dreaming about dogs, being an actress, and saving the world. Bea does spend some time on the stage, not acting, but speaking; shining a light on culture and human connection.

Recently Bea realized there are so many stories and experiences about dogs that can truly teach life lessons. Lessons about leadership, compassion, love, heartache, and unconditional love. Bea's passion for dogs leads her to believe we can learn more about connection and empathy just by hanging out with our furry friends. Bea wonders, how present are we to these learnings? And do we as humans truly understand a dog's purpose?

She will tell you the law of attraction works, especially when you least expect it. "When I was little, all I ever wanted was to be around dogs. I would bring home strays, hang out with anyone who had a dog, and beg my parents continuously for a dog of my own. I would dream of a place where I would be surrounded by hundreds of dogs." Today, the dream has come true in so many ways.

When Bea is not working on culture design and leadership, she supports her husband's company, The Leash Team. The purpose of this small family business is to create daily opportunities and special events where dogs can be dogs, and play, socialize and exercise together. The Leash Team is truly connecting and building something special in the community. If you want to see pure joy, check out @theleashteam on Instagram. Most importantly, Bea is surrounded by puppy love every day.

Bea is also a proud mother of two human children, Danielle and Liam, along with two fur babies, Buckley and Eddie. Bea has been married to her husband Dan for 30 years.

Manufactured by Amazon.ca
Bolton, ON

24028186R00103